ULTIMATE WEATHER-PEDIA

STEPHANIE WARREN DRIMMER

NATIONAL GEOGRAPHIC
WASHINGTON, D.C.

THE MOST COMPLETE WEATHER REFERENCE EVER

TABLE OF CONTENTS

Introduction 6
Foreword 7
Weather Wows! 8

Chapter 1:
The Wonder of Weather 10
Earth's Amazing Atmosphere 12
Sky Shows 14
It's All About Air 16
A Weather Recipe 18
Why Is Weather Important? 20

Chapter 2:
Watching the Weather 22
From Myth to Meteorology 24
Modern Meteorology:
    Measuring the Atmosphere 26
Modern Meteorology:
    Forecasting the Weather 28
Eyes in the Sky:
    Watching Weather From Above 30
Weather Wonders:
    Can Animals Predict the Weather? . . . 32
Follow That Storm!
    Interview With a Storm Chaser 34

Chapter 3:
Stormy Weather 36
Furious Forces:
    The 1900 Galveston Hurricane 38
What Is Rain? 40
Water From the Sky 42
Weather Wonders:
    What Is a Rainbow? 44
Clouds: Water in the Sky 46
Spooky Skyscape 48
Record Breakers: Hail 50
Shaped by Water 52
Thunderstorms 54
Zap! Lightning 56
Floods and Mudslides 58
Hurricanes 60

Chapter 4:
Windy Weather 62
Furious Forces:
    The Tri-State Tornado of 1925 64
What Is Wind? 66
Global Wind Patterns 68
Record Breakers:
    Highest Wind Speed 70
Tornadoes 72

Weather Wonders:
    How Can a Tornado Pick Up
    and Move Something as Huge
    as a House? 74
Monsoons 76
Shaped by Wind 78

Chapter 5:
Hot Weather 80
Furious Forces: Heat Wave 82
What Causes Hot Weather? 84
Record Breakers: Highest Heats 86
Too Hot:
    Strange Effects of Heat Waves 88
Weather Wonders:
    Can You Really Cook an Egg
    on the Sidewalk? 90
Too Dry: Drought 92
Dust Storms 94

Chapter 6:
Cold Weather 96
Furious Forces: "Snowmageddon" 98
What Makes Cold Weather? 100
Winter Wonderland 102
Record Breakers:
    The Coldest Place on Earth 104
Weather Wonders:
    How Does Cold Weather
    Preserve Mummies? 106
Blizzards 108
Ice Storms 110
Ancient Ice 112

Chapter 7:
Life in the Tropical Zone . . . 114
Climate in the Tropics 116
Survival Stories: Lost in the Amazon . . . 118
People in the Tropics 120
Making a Life:
    At Home in the Tropical Zone 122

Plants and Animals of the Tropics......124
Rain Renegade: Three-Toed Sloth 126
Shelter-Seeker:
    Blue Morpho Butterfly.............128
Super Sun-Soaker:
    Parson's Chameleon 130
Weather Wonders:
    What Do Animals Do When
    It Rains?.........................132
Slithering Snakes 134
Super Survivor: Collared Peccary 136
Wild About Water: Scarlet Macaw 138
On Top of the Tropics:
    Spider Monkey....................140

Chapter 8:
Life in the Desert Zones ... 142
Climate in the Desert 144
Survival Stories: Lost in the Desert....146
People in the Desert 148
Making a Life:
    At Home in the Desert Zones.......150
Weather Wonders:
    Where Did Sunscreen
    Come From? 152
Animals of the Desert................154
Heat-Releasing Ears: Fennec Fox......156
Adapted to Extremes:
    Bactrian Camel 158

Expert Water Harvester:
    Namib Desert Beetle..............160
Amazing Adaptations 162

Chapter 9:
Life at the Poles 164
Climate at the Poles 166
Survival Stories:
    Race to the South Pole............168
People in the Arctic 170
Making a Life:
    At Home in the North.............172
Weather Wonders:
    Why Doesn't Anyone Live
    in Antarctica?....................174
Animals at the Poles.................176
Extreme Cold Expert: Polar Bear 178
Feet for All Seasons: Caribou 180
Polar Plunge........................182
Feather Defense: Snowy Owl 184
Intelligent Insulation: Weddell Seal...186
Heat-Trapper: Adélie Penguin 188

Chapter 10:
Life in the Temperate Zone 190
Climate in the Temperate Zone 192
Survival Stories:
    Hiking the Appalachian Trail 194
People in the Temperate Zone 196
Making a Life:
    At Home in the Temperate Zone....198
Weather Wonders:
    Why Is the Sky Blue? 200
Animals in the Temperate Zone.......202
Slowing Down to Survive:
    Brown Bear 204
They Come Out at Night.............206
Marvelous Migrator:
    Monarch Butterfly................208

Hiding in Plain Sight:
    Snowshoe Hare...................210
Supersize Sun-Seeker:
    American Alligator 212
Snow-Stalker: Red Fox..............214

Chapter 11:
Weather and Climate
Change.................... 216
Warming World 218
Changing Climate, Changing Planet ... 220
An Extreme Future 222
Animals and Climate Change 224
Humans and Climate Change.........226
Disappearing Places.................228
Stepping Up........................ 230

Chapter 12:
Wild Weather 232
You're Seeing Things: Mirages........ 234
Sparks in the Sky: St. Elmo's Fire 236
Weird Water Weather 238
Spinning Flames: Fire Tornadoes 240
Extreme Electricity:
    Lightning Phenomena............. 242
Rainbows at Night: Moonbows........ 244
What's Up There? Rare Clouds........ 246

Chapter 13:
Space Weather 248
Survival Stories: Apollo 13 250
Strange Solar System 252
Loony Lunar Effects: Far-Out Moons .. 254
Wacky Moon Weather............... 256
Wild Worlds: Exoplanets 258

Glossary........................... 262
Find Out More...................... 264
Index.............................. 265
Photo & Illustration Credits........... 270
Credits 272

INTRODUCTION

Dark clouds gather overhead. A few raindrops fall, then more. Thunder rumbles in the distance.

Snow falls silently, covering the ground in a fluffy white blanket and turning a town into a scene from a holiday card.

High winds whip sand into a wall thousands of feet high. Sand moves across the desert, covering everything in its path in a dark cloud.

All over the world, people start their day by looking out the window to see what the weather will be like. But weather is about so much more than deciding if you should carry an umbrella with you. Weather can be a cool breeze or a warm day. It can be a beautiful rainbow or a stunning sunset. It can also be a raging hurricane, a violent tornado, or a deadly heat wave.

Ancient people thought that mysterious powers were behind weather events. If floods or heat waves destroyed their crops, they believed the gods were angry. Today, we know that weather is caused by a combination of natural forces all interacting together that change from moment to moment and from place to place. We can now measure weather and predict it. But we still can't control it. Weather can make for the perfect ski vacation, or it can destroy an entire town.

And weather doesn't just affect humans. All animals, from fluttering butterflies to majestic polar bears, must deal with the changing weather. Many have incredible adaptations that help them survive weather extremes from storms to drought.

If you've ever wondered how weather works, this book is for you. You'll follow a raindrop on a journey around the planet and talk to a storm chaser who gets up close and personal with wild weather. Ready for the adventure? Read on—but you might want to bring an umbrella, just in case!

Stephanie Warren Drimmer,
science writer and author
of *Ultimate Weatherpedia*

FOREWORD

I have a pretty cool job: I'm an atmospheric scientist. That means I study the Earth's atmosphere and its weather. But my main focus is severe storms!

While most people are running away from whipping winds and spinning cyclones, I am running toward them. Why? Because I want to learn more about what is happening inside these furious forces.

I didn't know this would be my job, but I did know that I liked nature, technology, and physics. To me, the stranger or bigger or more extreme something was—whether it was a skyscraper or a bolt of lightning— the more fascinating it was. Tornadoes, hurricanes, and other weather phenomena were so exciting and so unknown to me, I had to learn more.

Everyone cares about the weather because it impacts their day ... every day. Sunny, windy, rainy— what greets you when you step outside into the world matters a lot. To understand weather's extremes, you need to understand its building blocks—the fundamentals. Meteorology, the study of weather, relies on integrating knowledge from so many different fields—computers, physics, chemistry, mathematics, and engineering—to know more about how the weather works.

And there is still so much to discover about the weather! This book is a great resource to learn about what weather is and how it impacts life all over the world. So be curious, jump in, and enjoy exploring all things weather!

Karen Kosiba,
atmospheric scientist at the
Center for Severe Weather
Research in Boulder, Colorado

WEATHER
WOWS!

A bolt of lightning can travel through the air at up to 224,000 miles an hour (360,000 km/h) and reach temperatures of 54,032°F (30,000°C). That's hotter than the surface of the sun!

Thunderstorms that produce clumped balls of ice are called hailstorms. Hailstones about an inch (2.5 cm) or larger are usually big enough to cause damage to cars and other surfaces. In 2010, hail the size of grapefruit fell in South Dakota, U.S.A.!

If all the ice in the Antarctic melted, the oceans would rise by about 216 feet (66 m)—taller than the height of a 20-story building!

Thinking of visiting Yuma, Arizona, U.S.A.? You'll probably be there on a sunny day! Yuma is the sunniest place on Earth. It receives more than 4,000 sunlight hours per year—the most of any city in the world.

A cricket can tell you the temperature! If you count the number of chirps a cricket makes in 14 seconds and then add 40, you'll have a rough idea of the outside temperature in degrees Fahrenheit (°F).

The whirling winds inside a tornado can reach 298 miles an hour (480 km/h), fast enough to blow the roofs off buildings, tear trees out of the ground by the roots, and even fling cars hundreds of feet.

You don't have to wait for rain to (hopefully!) spot a rainbow! Rainbows can also be seen in fog, spray, mist, and dew.

Tornadoes can appear over water! Some, called tornadic waterspouts, begin as land tornadoes that then move out over water. Others, known as fair weather waterspouts, develop on the surface of the water. Super hot steam plumes from volcanic eruptions can also spawn waterspouts.

CHAPTER 1
THE WONDER OF WEATHER

Weather shapes how all living things survive on planet Earth. Tornadoes, snowfall, and dust storms are powerful forces of nature that can destroy homes and lives. But weather is not just extreme events: It's part of our everyday lives. Sunny days, gentle breezes, cool rain showers—these are all weather, too. Weather affects us all the time, from what we decide to wear to where we choose to live. But what exactly *is* weather?

All of Earth's weather comes from the sun. Even though the sun is really far away, it's also really hot: nearly 10,000°F (5600°C) at its surface! Some of that heat reaches all the way to planet Earth, warming its surface. But the sun doesn't heat Earth evenly. Sunlight hits the planet at different angles during different times of the day and the year. And Earth's surface varies from place to place: Some areas have oceans, while others have deserts or huge mountain ranges. So some parts of Earth's surface heat up a lot, while others heat up just a little. All weather on Earth is a result of this uneven heating. From a heat wave to a cold snap, it's all because of the sun!

EARTH'S AMAZING ATMOSPHERE

Weather is what's happening in the air. And another word for air is atmosphere: the layer of gases that surrounds Earth. Without the atmosphere, there would be no weather.

The atmosphere is all around you, but you can't see it unless you look at Earth from space. This image (below right) shows how the edge of our planet looks from orbit. This surface is covered with white clouds, and the moon hangs in the distance. But what's that strange blue haze in the middle? That's the atmosphere!

The atmosphere acts like a blanket. It keeps Earth at a comfortable temperature, protecting us from the freezing temperatures of space and the scorching heat and harmful rays from the sun. It also helps keep Earth safe from objects hurtling through space, such as meteors. When these objects come close to our planet, they usually burn up in the atmosphere instead of striking the surface.

But, unlike a blanket, the atmosphere doesn't just sit there. The air that makes up the atmosphere is always moving from one place to another. Earth's sunlight, water, and surface topography—such as mountains and deserts—all change the way air moves around the planet. This movement of air creates clouds, rain, storms, and everything else we call weather. All these forces act together, making weather hard to predict. No wonder the weather report is sometimes wrong!

Bet You Didn't Know!

Earth had almost no atmosphere when it formed about 4.6 billion years ago

LAYERS OF THE ATMOSPHERE

Like a cake, Earth's atmosphere is made up of different
layers stacked on top of one another.

EXOSPHERE
Thermosphere to 6,200 miles
(10,000 km)

In the outermost layer, the exosphere,
Earth's atmosphere merges with outer
space. The air is incredibly thin here:
Atoms and molecules are so far apart
that they can travel hundreds of miles
without running into each other. The
temperatures are at absolute zero, the
lowest possible.

THERMOSPHERE
Mesosphere to 621 miles
(1,000 km)

In the thermosphere, sunlight heats
up individual gas molecules to 3600°F
(2000°C). But because the air molecules in the thermosphere are so far
apart, this layer would feel super cold
to us! Satellites orbit here.

MESOSPHERE
Stratosphere to 53 miles
(85 km)

In the mesosphere, gases are thick
enough to slow down meteors that
zip into the Earth's atmosphere from
space. They burn up, leaving bright
trails in the night sky that we call
shooting stars.

STRATOSPHERE
Troposphere to 30 miles
(50 km)

Airplanes cruise in the lower part of
the stratosphere.

TROPOSPHERE
Earth's surface to 6.2 miles (10 km)

Most weather happens in the troposphere, the part of
Earth's atmosphere that is closest to the ground. It begins
at Earth's surface and extends up about 6.2 miles (10 km).

13

SKY SHOWS

It protects Earth and provides the air you breathe. But did you know that the atmosphere is also responsible for some of the most dazzling light displays on the planet? Here are a few of the atmosphere's most astounding acts.

AURORAS

At Earth's poles, mysterious, colorful lights sometimes seem to take over the whole sky. These auroras occur when huge storms on the sun send tiny particles of energy speeding toward Earth. When those particles, attracted by our planet's strong magnetic field, collide with the gases in our atmosphere, they release light. Different gases give off different colors: Some are green, some pink, some violet.

Earth is not the only planet in our solar system with auroras. Gas giants Jupiter, Saturn, Uranus, and Neptune have them, too.

SHOOTING STARS

These streaks of light moving across the night sky aren't stars at all. They are actually bits of space rock called meteorites hurtling through space at tens of thousands of miles an hour. When they hit the atmosphere, they heat up so much that they catch on fire! Most burn up until there is nothing left.

SPRITES AND ELVES

No, we're not referring to miniature supernatural beings. *These* sprites and elves are bright flashes of light that occur high in Earth's atmosphere and are associated with thunderstorms. They were first spotted by airline pilots, who noticed them while flying over extreme thunderstorms. Scientists began studying them in the 1990s, along with another type of flash called jets. The details about how they are formed are still a mystery.

SUNSETS

Almost everybody has watched as the sun sinks below the horizon, sending brilliant colors spreading across the sky. But not everyone realizes that Earth wouldn't have its spectacular sunsets without the atmosphere! As the sun sinks, its rays travel in long curved paths along the edge of Earth. They pass through 40 times more air than they do at midday. Particles in the atmosphere, such as dust and water droplets, scatter and absorb blue and green light, enhancing the reds, yellows, and golds.

15

Wind helps move these sailboats in San Francisco Bay, California, U.S.A.

IT'S ALL ABOUT AIR

It doesn't feel like it, but air is heavy. In fact, you've got 1.1 tons (1 t) of air pressing down on you right now—the weight of a small car!

Like every other substance, air is made up of tiny particles called molecules. Imagine that air molecules are like a group of cheerleaders forming a human pyramid. The cheerleaders at the bottom have to bear the weight of all the people stacked on top of them. And the cheerleader at the very top has no weight on his or her shoulders.

The atmosphere works the same way: Down near Earth's surface, the air is weighed down by all the air above it. That pressure squeezes those air molecules close together. The squeezing of those air molecules creates high air pressure in the bottom part of the atmosphere. At the top of the atmosphere, there's very little pressing down on the air molecules. Molecules high in the atmosphere are much farther apart, and the air pressure is very low.

Temperature can change air pressure. When air is warmed up, its pressure decreases. Its molecules move faster, causing them to move farther apart. Because there is more space between the molecules, the warm air is less dense than the surrounding air, so it rises.

When air cools down, its pressure increases. Its molecules move more slowly, causing them to move closer together. Because there is less space between the molecules, the cold air is more dense than the air around it, so it sinks. Air warmed by the sun rises, and when it does, cool air often moves in to fill the empty space. That movement of air from areas of high pressure to areas of lower pressure is what we call wind.

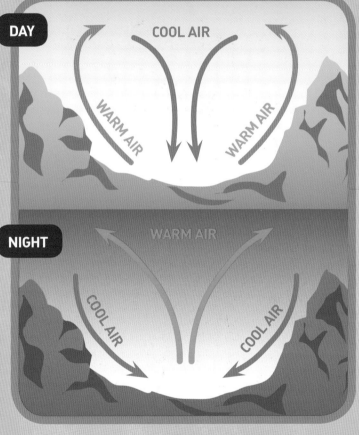

TEMPERATURE AND AIR MOVEMENT

DAY

COOL AIR

WARM AIR

WARM AIR

NIGHT

WARM AIR

COOL AIR

COOL AIR

Bet You Didn't Know!

People will tell you that air is made up of oxygen. But that's only partly true: A mere 21 percent of air is actually oxygen. Most of it—about 78 percent—is nitrogen. The rest is made of tiny amounts of other gases such as carbon dioxide, hydrogen, and argon.

A WEATHER RECIPE

If you want to cook up changes in the weather, you need three main ingredients: sunlight, moving air, and water.

STEP ONE: *Heat Earth's surface.*

When the sun rises each morning, it warms the ground, oceans, trees, and buildings. When air touches these sun-warmed surfaces, the molecules in the air absorb the heat. The warm molecules move away from each other, causing the air to expand and become less dense, or lighter. This lighter air floats upward. It's the same principle that powers a hot-air balloon: Fire heats up the air inside the balloon, making it rise into the sky.

STEP TWO: *Sprinkle in water.*

Earth is a watery world—71 percent of our surface is water! The sun shines on the water molecules in Earth's soil, rivers, lakes, and oceans. When these water molecules absorb the sun's heat energy, they turn into a gas called water vapor, or steam. This gas rises with the warming air. High in the sky, the water vapor cools, making water droplets. When lots of droplets gather together, they form clouds that release the water as rain, snow, hail, or sleet.

STEP THREE: *Swirl the air.*

On Earth, air never stops moving. As air warmed by the sun rises high above Earth's surface, it cools. As it cools, its molecules move closer together. That makes the air dense, or heavy. This denser air sinks to the ground, where it warms up again, and the cycle repeats. This circular movement of air creates wind. Wind is its own type of weather, and it also moves other weather, such as rainstorms, from one place to another. Wind carries heat and water all around the planet.

SUNLIGHT & WATER

Water vapor cools and condenses, creating clouds.

Water absorbs the sun's heat, turns into vapor, and rises with the warming air.

Heavy clouds release water as rain, snow, hail, or sleet.

SUNLIGHT & AIR

High above, the air cools down again and becomes heavier.

The sun warms air on Earth's surface; warmed air rises.

Cooled, heavy air sinks down to Earth.

WHY IS WEATHER IMPORTANT?

Earth's weather is a powerful force.

Severe weather events—blizzards and sizzling summers, tornadoes and hurricanes—can cause disasters that take a toll on human life. But though weather can sometimes be violent, it's also vital for all life on Earth.

All life as we know it—from the teeniest microbe to the biggest blue whale—needs water to survive. And it's weather that carries this water all around Earth. Water cycles from Earth's surface up into the sky to become clouds. Winds push those clouds all over the planet, where they release their water in new places. Without weather to move water around, our planet's land would dry up into a wasteland where nothing could live.

Most living things also need just the right amount of the sun's heat to survive. Differences in temperature create wind, which carries heat energy from one place to another, circulating it around Earth's surface. That process provides warmth to living creatures all around the planet.

Different places on Earth have different long-term weather patterns, called climates. Life depends on that weather variety, too. The rainforest's warm temperatures and constant rain, for example, make great conditions for plants to grow. These plants provide much of the world's oxygen supply, providing air for people and animals to breathe. The icy poles act like Earth's thermostat, helping cool down ocean water from the topics and keeping our planet from overheating.

This vast variety of weather also means that different parts of Earth are hopping, swimming, and flying with all kinds of different creatures. Camels find a perfect home in the heat of the Sahara desert, and polar bears feel just right in the chill of the Arctic. It's the same for monkeys and meerkats, sand cats and snowy owls—and you. Earth's incredible diversity wouldn't be possible without the perpetual dance of heat, wind, and water.

It's wild, it's wonderful—it's weather!

WEATHER VS. CLIMATE

Weather and climate are related, but they're not the same thing. The difference is time: Weather is what's happening in the short term, from the next few minutes to the next few months. Climate, on the other hand, is the long-term weather patterns in a particular area. One way to remember it is that climate is what you expect, such as cold winters in the northern United States. And weather is what you get, like a blizzard that's predicted to happen tomorrow.

A landspout tornado spins across a field in Kansas, U.S.A.

CHAPTER 2
WATCHING THE WEATHER

Look up at the sky. Right away you can tell whether it's sunny, stormy, or snowing—but what will the weather be like tomorrow? What about next week or next month? Humans have been trying to predict the weather for thousands of years. But forecasting is no easy feat: The complex interplay of air, water, and wind is incredibly difficult to decipher. Modern meteorologists use cutting-edge technology to monitor the world's weather patterns and try to foresee how they'll change in the future. Here's how they do it.

Storm chaser and scientist Robin Tanamachi deploys the University of Massachusetts mobile W-band radar near a hail-producing Iowa thunderstorm in 2009.

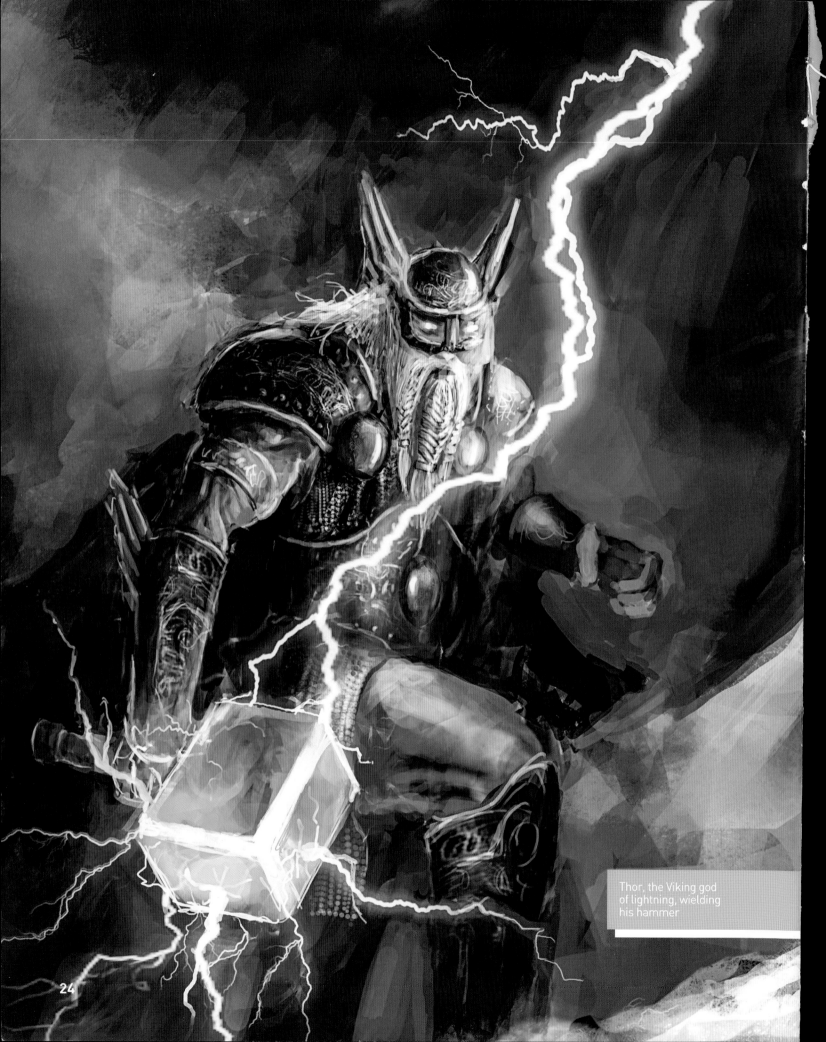

Thor, the Viking god of lightning, wielding his hammer

FROM MYTH TO METEOROLOGY

Before scientists discovered ways to understand the weather, people told stories to make sense of events such as storms, seasons, winds, and rainbows.

Ancient Scandinavians believed that lightning was really a spark flying from the mighty hammer of Thor, king of the Norse gods (depicted on the opposite page)—and that thunder was the sound of his chariot crossing the sky. The ancient Greeks believed that winter happened when one of their goddesses, Persephone, was forced to live in the underworld for part of every year. And the Native American Kiowa people believed tornadoes were created when a supernatural being they called Storm-Maker Red Horse whipped his long, snake-like tail through the air.

In ancient times, people watched the weather closely for clues about when to plant and harvest. Too early or too late, and their crops could fail and people could starve. Sudden hailstorms or heat waves could devastate farmland, too. Researchers recently discovered what they believe could be one of the world's oldest weather reports: a stone slab with carvings that described the weather 3,500 years ago in Egypt.

An ancient Greek scientist named Aristotle was one of the first people to study what makes weather change. Around 340 B.C., he wrote a book called *Meteorology*, which discussed theories about the formation of rain, hail, clouds, wind, hurricanes, thunder, and lightning. Although he got a few things right, many of his ideas were wrong. But his text was considered to be the authority on weather for almost 2,000 years.

Starting in the 15th century, early scientists began making scientific observations to understand the weather. They invented new instruments for measuring properties of the atmosphere such as moisture, temperature, and pressure. It was the beginning of meteorology, the study of weather.

Bet You Didn't Know!

We still have myths about weather. Every year on February 2, people in the United States celebrate Groundhog Day. But that groundhog, named Punxsutawney Phil, is no meteorologist: In his 30 predictions between 1988 and 2017, he accurately forecast winter's end only six times.

MODERN METEOROLOGY:
MEASURING THE ATMOSPHERE

As people developed new tools for analyzing the conditions of the atmosphere, meteorology turned from a guessing game into a science.

1714

Polish-born Dutch physicist Daniel Fahrenheit developed the mercury thermometer, the first really precise way to measure temperature.

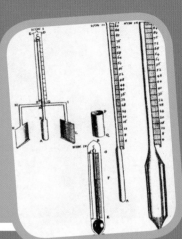

1600   1650   1700   1750   1800

1643

Italian physicist Evangelista Torricelli realized that changes in air pressure were connected to changes in weather. He invented the barometer to measure air pressure.

1837

Weather scientists weren't able to share data while weather was happening until American inventor Samuel Morse came up with the telegraph. For the first time, meteorologists could share information and use it to create the first weather maps.

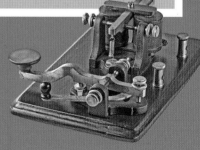

1910s

Norwegian meteorologists led by father and son Vilhelm and Jacob Bjerknes developed the concepts of air masses and fronts. They used the laws of physics to figure out that huge cold and warm air masses move in predictable patterns.

1950s

With the invention of computers, meteorologists had a way to analyze massive amounts of data and produce the first models of atmospheric conditions. These models could predict how weather systems would move around the globe.

1850   1900   1950   2000

WORLD WARS I (1914–1918) AND II (1939–1945)

The ability to attack under the cover of clouds or march when the weather is fair can mean the difference between an army's success or failure. During the two World Wars, the ability to predict weather all over the globe suddenly became hugely important. All kinds of new technologies were developed during this period, including radar.

1962

The first meteorological satellite, TIROS-I, provided the first accurate weather forecast from space. TIROS-I gave meteorologists the ability to collect and transmit data with extreme accuracy. Today, satellites and computers are the most important tools of modern meteorologists.

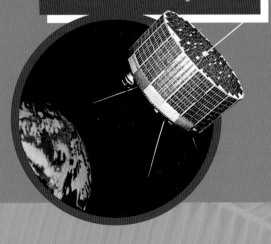

MODERN METEOROLOGY:
FORECASTING THE WEATHER

Should I bring an umbrella with me today? Will it be hot this weekend? What should I pack for my vacation next month? We rely on weather predictions all the time.

To create weather forecasts, meteorologists collect information, or data, about the current state of the atmosphere using many different measuring tools (see pages 30–31). Data from thousands of weather stations across the globe are gathered and pooled together. Then, meteorologists use the principles of physics—mathematics that explains natural processes, like how air moves around the globe—to predict how the state of the atmosphere will change as time moves forward.

All the weather-related sensors and gauges on Earth produce a lot of data: more than one million weather-related observations every day! An ordinary household computer wouldn't be able to process all that data. Meteorologists use powerful supercomputers that take in these weather observations and feed them into mathematical equations based on the physics that control how the atmosphere changes. These models project how the weather might look in the future and are the basis of weather forecasts.

Predicting the weather accurately is an enormous challenge. There are countless factors that meteorologists must consider, from how the sun will heat Earth's surface to how differences in air pressure will form winds to how those winds will move around the globe. Small changes in any one of these factors can dramatically affect future weather. And there are still factors that experts don't yet completely understand. All of this means there's a limit to how accurate weather predictions can be. No wonder the weather forecast isn't always correct!

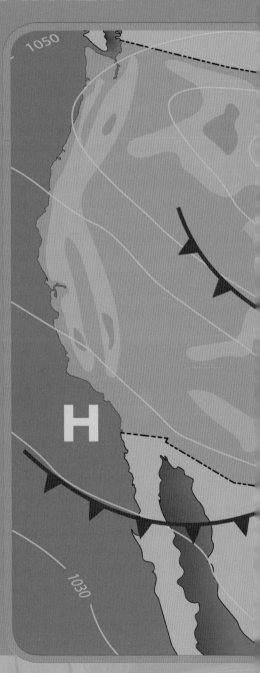

HOW TO READ A WEATHER MAP

If you've ever watched a television weather forecast, you've probably seen a weather map like this one. Words like "rain" and "snow" are easy to understand—but what do all those strange symbols mean?

WARM FRONT

These strings of red half-circles show the transition zone where a mass of warm air moves in to replace cold air. The half circles point in the direction of the cold air that will be replaced. A warm front often brings precipitation such as rain, snow, and sleet.

H AND L

These symbols show areas of high and low surface pressure. Low pressure systems lead to rising air, and high pressure systems lead to sinking air.

COLD FRONT

This is the transition area where a mass of cold air moves in to replace a mass of warm air. The triangles point in the direction of the warm air that will be replaced. Cold fronts can bring colder temperatures, precipitation, and high wind speeds.

STATIONARY FRONT

This sting of blue triangles and red half-circles shows a zone where a cold and a warm front meet and then neither moves out of the way. Stationary fronts bring long periods of rain that stay in one spot.

OCCLUDED FRONT

In one common type of front, a cold front moves faster than a warm front and can sometimes catch up and overtake the warm front, usually bringing precipitation. That's called an occluded front, drawn as a purple line with both half circles and triangles that point in the direction the front is moving.

EYES IN THE SKY: WATCHING WEATHER FROM ABOVE

Meteorologists have a lot of different ways to gather information about global weather events. Scientists around the world share images and data they've gathered … sometimes from very far above the ground!

WEATHER PLANE WITH RADAR

Hurricane hunters are a special breed of pilots who fly planes into hurricanes. The planes carry sensors that send details about pressure, wind direction, wind speed, and sea temperature. Hurricane hunters also drop radiosondes as they fly. Today, unmanned drones are beginning to do this work so pilots no longer have to risk their lives to gather data.

ISS

The International Space Station (ISS) helps monitor stormy weather from 220 miles (350 km) up. Video of spiraling hurricanes from the ISS offers meteorologists front-row seats to these events. They can see how the clouds are moving and how their shapes are changing, helping them forecast future weather events.

WEATHER BALLOON AND RADIOSONDE

Huge weather balloons lift a sensor called a radiosonde more than 22 miles (35 km) above Earth. The radiosonde transmits details about air pressure, temperature, water vapor, wind direction, and speed to scientists on the ground.

WHAT IS RADAR?

Radar works by transmitting radio signals in a certain direction, then "listening" for the echoes of any signals that bounce off objects in their path. It was originally developed to detect aircraft and ships, but people realized that their radar systems were detecting storms, too. Radar can detect not only the location and intensity of precipitation, but also the movement of air within a storm. It does that by using a principle called the Doppler effect, a change in the returning radio waves caused by objects in motion Today, radar technology helps meteorologists predict storms with greater accuracy.

RADAR

On the ground, radar creates a weather picture by bouncing bursts of microwave energy off raindrops, dust, snowflakes, bugs, and anything else that is in the atmosphere.

31

CAN ANIMALS PREDICT THE WEATHER?

If you've ever had your dog come running inside just before a downpour hits, you might have wondered, _Do animals know something about the weather that we don't?_

There are all kinds of tales about animals acting odd before weather events. Some say sheep huddle together before it rains or frogs croak loudly when a storm is approaching. But is it really possible that these creatures can sense what's about to happen? It's difficult for scientists to test whether animals make weather forecasts. But there are a few documented cases of animals getting out of the way before storms strike.

In 2014, scientists were monitoring the migration of a group of birds called golden-winged warblers when they noticed something odd. Seemingly out of nowhere, the birds abandoned their breeding grounds in Tennessee, U.S.A., and winged it for Florida. A few days later, a large, severe thunderstorm struck the area the warblers had just left. After the storm

passed, the birds flew back to Tennessee, having traveled more than 900 miles (1,500 km) round-trip to escape the weather.

Something similar had happened in 2001, when 14 blacktip sharks that scientists were observing with radio trackers swam into deeper waters just before tropical storm Gabrielle made landfall in Terra Ceia Bay in Florida. Then again, when Hurricane Charley approached in 2004, six out of eight radio-tagged sharks in the area moved out of the way. (The other two sharks swam out of range of the equipment, and therefore their movements could not be monitored.)

What was going on? Scientists don't know for sure, but they have a theory: Many animals have an ability to sense changes in the environment around them that people don't have. For example, while humans are able to hear sounds that are in the range of 20 hertz to 20,000 kilohertz (a hertz is a measure of a sound's frequency, which determines how high- or low-pitched a sound is), some creatures, such as dogs, elephants, and bats, can hear sounds well beyond that range. Storms produce a type of sound called infrasound too low for human ears to detect. Scientists think that maybe animals like the warblers and sharks got out of the way because they could hear the storm coming. And it's also possible they can sense other changes—such as slight drops in air or water pressure—that signal a storm's approach.

Experts are just beginning to investigate how animals might detect oncoming weather. Someday, what they learn might help them make better predictions about when storms are on the way and where they'll strike. But until then, you're probably better watching the Weather Channel than asking your dog for the forecast!

Bet You Didn't Know!

Scientists have noticed that certain fish seem to prefer water that is around 80°F (26.5°C)—the same exact temperature at which tropical storms form. Some scientists are now tracking fish in the Gulf of Mexico to see if they can use their movement to help predict hurricanes.

GOLDEN-WINGED WARBLER

FOLLOW THAT STORM!

INTERVIEW WITH A STORM CHASER

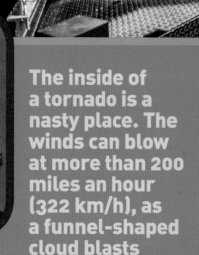

The inside of a tornado is a nasty place. The winds can blow at more than 200 miles an hour (322 km/h), as a funnel-shaped cloud blasts along the ground wrecking everything in its path. So why would someone want to get inside this whirling cone of destruction? Science, of course!

Robin Tanamachi is a meteorologist at Purdue University in Indiana, U.S.A. She's also a storm chaser who gets up close and personal with howling winds and pelting rain. Here's what she says about her work.

Q: Were you always interested in weather?
A: Ever since I can remember, I was fascinated by weather. I would lie in the grass and watch the clouds. I was curious about thunderstorms and fog. I was always trying to figure out what was happening around me.

Q: How old were you when you decided to become a weather scientist?

A: In 1986, when I was seven years old, there was a TV helicopter flyer reporting news in my home-town of Minneapolis, Minnesota (that's where I grew up). During the report, a tornado dropped down in front of the helicopter as it was in the air. The crew flew after the tornado and broadcast it live on TV from start to finish.

Within a few days, there was a TV special about the tornado. Weather scientists were interviewed from the National Severe Storms Laboratory in Norman, Oklahoma. That was the first time I heard of a severe storm lab or a scientist who studied tornadoes. That was it: I wanted to become a research meteorologist.

Q: What does a storm chaser do?

A: Most of my time is spent sitting at a computer, analyzing data and writing papers. But for one or two months per year, it is really exciting. The severe weather season in Oklahoma is April to June. In Indiana it's May to July. My team is basically on call during that season. We have a team of three people: a driver, a navigator, and a radar operator. Before we head out, we make a forecast to see the chance of severe weather in our area. If we find something, we drive the radar truck to the target area. I've driven 600 miles (966 km) for a storm. We find six to eight storms in a season. About a quarter of the time they become tornadoes. But no matter what, we always take radar measurements.

Q: How do you know if a thunder-storm might become a tornado?

A: There's no way to know for sure. There are four "ingredients" that we look for in a target area. We look for shear (changes in wind speed or direction), lift, instability, and moisture in the air. Using radar and satellite images from the National Weather Service, we find thunderstorms that are rotating, called supercells. We look for a hook forming off to one side—that's the spot where a tornado may form.

Q: What is it like to chase a storm? Have you had any close calls?

A: I've had a few close scrapes. You have to look around 360 degrees all the time. If there is a tornado in front of you, there might also be one behind you. One night, we could see the tornado only when lightning lit it up. Then it was dark for a while, and we lost it. We hadn't seen it for a few minutes and then suddenly we got side-swiped and blasted with gravel. The vehicle behind us got its windows blown out. Luckily, nobody was hurt.

Q: What tips do you have for kids who might want to become storm chasers when they grow up?

A: Kids who want to get involved in severe weather spotting should go to a free training session through a local office of the National Weather Service (NWS). Meteorologists teach you what features of a storm might look like a tornado but aren't. They can also teach you how to report what you are seeing to the NWS accurately. Kids as young as five can do that!

OPPOSITE: Robin Tanamachi secures the University of Massachusetts mobile W-band Doppler radar dish in southwestern Iowa, U.S.A.

CHAPTER 3
STORMY WEATHER

The sky darkens. The winds pick up, and clouds roll in. A storm is coming. This disturbance of the atmosphere is accompanied by strong winds and often rain, thunder, lightning, or snow. Some storms are gentle, just enough to wash the pavement down and make the trees look fresh and green. Other times, storms can turn severe, zapping the ground with bolts of lightning, sending extreme rain that causes floods and mudslides, and even forming deadly hurricanes. Storms are one of nature's most powerful weather events.

A supercell thunderstorm produces
cloud-to-ground lightning in eastern
South Dakota, U.S.A.

THE 1900 GALVESTON HURRICANE

The hurricane season of 2017 was one of the most destructive on record. After 12 years without a major hurricane hitting the United States ("major" meaning category 3 or higher), Hurricane Harvey slammed into the central Texas coast on August 25. A few weeks later, Hurricane Irma hit the U.S. Virgin Islands and then Florida. Then came Hurricane Maria just over a week later, making landfall in the U.S. territory of Puerto Rico. The triple hurricanes brought widespread death and destruction and caused more than $200 billion in damage.

But as terrible as these hurricanes were, they weren't as bad as the Galveston hurricane of 1900.

At the dawn of the 20th century, Galveston was a bustling city on a low-lying island off the coast of mainland Texas. Known as the "Jewel of Texas," it was the state's most developed city, with the largest port, the most millionaires, and the first telephones and electric lights. More than 40,000 people lived there, and many more enjoyed the summer seasons by visiting the beaches there. But everything changed on September 8, 1900, when a monster hurricane hit. Winds blew faster than 135 miles an hour (217 km/h), and the seas rose by

The Galveston hurricane was the single deadliest natural disaster in American history.

ABOVE: An illustration depicting the hurricane's destruction appeared in the French newspaper *Le Petit Parisien* in 1900.

TOP RIGHT: People use ropes to clear debris after the Galveston hurricane.

15 feet (4.6 m)—far above the city's highest points. The island was destroyed. Within hours, between 6,000 and 12,000 people were dead, and 30,000—three-quarters of the entire population of the city—were homeless.

After the storm, the U.S. Army Corps of Engineers constructed a 17-foot (5.2-m) wall to hold back the sea. It lifted 2,000 surviving buildings and pumped sand underneath them. Residents tried to rebuild their homes and their lives, but Galveston never returned to its former glory.

One positive thing did come out of the terrible tragedy: It made people realize they had to figure out a way to predict future storms. Before Galveston, people relied on spotty information from whatever ships happened to be in the Gulf of Mexico. The citizens of Galveston could tell a storm was brewing, but because they had no warning of how dangerous it would be, they had no way to prepare.

Today, the National Hurricane Center detects oncoming storms, tracks their progress, and predicts where they will go next. It uses satellites to watch storms as they form and powerful computers to create accurate forecasts. Then, it issues warnings for dangerous storms so that people have time to get to safety. During the 2017 hurricane season, people in Texas watched as Harvey approached for nearly a week before it hit, and Puerto Rico declared a state of emergency two days before Irma. Advance notice doesn't keep storms from becoming disasters, however—three months after the hurricane, 45 percent of Puerto Ricans still had no power and 14 percent had no tap water—but it's an important tool in helping to prevent tragedies on the scale of the Galveston hurricane from happening again in the future.

WHAT IS RAIN?

During 2017's Hurricane Harvey, a record-breaking amount of rain fell on the Gulf Coast. Scientists calculate that over six days, about 27 trillion gallons (102 trillion L) of water fell. That's about one million gallons (3.8 million L) for every person in Texas! While some storms produce torrential rains, others can create heavy snow or crushing hail. This precipitation, the last step in a process that moves water around and around Earth, is called the water cycle. Here's how it works.

THE WATER CYCLE

COLLECTION

Precipitation that falls on land will soak through the soil and collect as underground water. Earth's gravity pulls it into streams, rivers, lakes, and the ocean. There, the sun heats it up—starting the water cycle all over again.

PRECIPITATION

Sometimes, the tiny water droplets that make up a cloud collide with each other. They squish together, forming bigger water droplets. Eventually, those water droplets get so big and heavy that the cloud can no longer hold them. They fall to the ground as precipitation: rain, snow, hail, or sleet.

CONDENSATION

Water vapor rises high into the sky. And just like air does whenever it rises, the water vapor cools. It turns back into a liquid, forming clouds. The winds that blow high up in the atmosphere move these clouds, helping water travel all around the globe.

EVAPORATION

Energy from the sun—in the form of heat—warms up the water in our rivers, lakes, and oceans. It breaks the bonds that hold some of the water molecules together, making the water change from a liquid into a gas called water vapor. (It's the same thing that fogs up the bathroom mirror when you take a shower!)

41

WATER FROM THE SKY

Unless rain is falling from the sky, we usually don't think about it. But if you live in the United States, there are 40 trillion gallons (151 trillion L) of water lingering above your head at any given moment! Every day, about four trillion (13 trillion L) of those gallons fall to Earth. Sometimes this precipitation is rain; other times it's snow, sleet, or hail. What's going on up in the sky to make this happen?

The process starts when warm, moist air rises into the sky. As it goes, it cools. If it cools to its dew point—the temperature at which it can't hold any more water—it can condense, turning into liquid water and forming clouds. But most of the time, condensation can only happen if there are tiny particles floating in the air for water to stick to. These particles can be bits of dust from the highway, soot from a wood fire, sea salt from the ocean, or sometimes, ice crystals.

Tiny water droplets collect on these particles, then come together in bigger water droplets, eventually falling as rain. If the air is lifted high enough into the air, where the temperature is below freezing, the moisture may form ice crystals. When these ice crystals form in a special cloud called a supercooled cloud (which contains liquid water droplets that temporarily reach temperatures below zero degrees Celsius), they become snow crystals. As these snow crystals fall into lower, warmer air, they join together with other snow crystals, forming snowflakes.

If moist air forms raindrops but is then carried into a below-freezing zone, it becomes hail or a type of frozen precipitation called graupel. If rain drops pass through a layer of cold air on their way to the ground, they become sleet. And if rain stays liquid until it reaches frozen ground, then suddenly freezes on impact, it's known as freezing rain, or glaze. Freezing rain can coat roads, power lines, and trees with a slick coating of ice, creating dangerous conditions.

HOW MUCH WATER?

If you packed together all the water in our atmosphere, rivers, oceans, groundwater, and everywhere else, it would form a sphere that is only about 860 miles (1,384 km) wide—the distance between the U.S. cities of Salt Lake City, Utah, and Topeka, Kansas.

That sphere gets even smaller when you only count the water we can drink. Only one percent of Earth's water is liquid freshwater found in rivers, lakes, and groundwater. If you packed all of Earth's drinkable water into a sphere, it would be only about 170 miles (274 km) wide—less than the distance between New York City and Boston, Massachusetts.

The image below compares the volume of the planet with the relative amounts of water on Earth. The largest water sphere represents the volume of all of Earth's water; the medium-size drop represents all the world's liquid freshwater (99 percent of it groundwater, a lot of it is not accessible to people); and the smallest droplet represents the freshwater in all the lakes and rivers on the planet (accessible, surface-water sources).

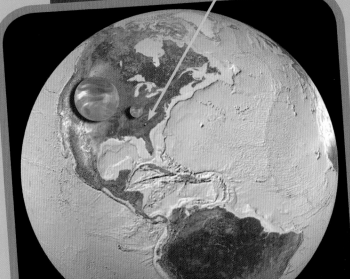

WHAT IS A RAINBOW?

The ancient Greeks believed the sight of a rainbow in the sky signaled that Iris, a messenger between the mortals and the gods, was passing by, wearing her multicolored robes. Ancient Polynesians thought a rainbow was a ladder that their heroes used to climb up to heaven. And in Norse mythology, a rainbow connects Earth with Asgard, where the gods live. You might not believe these old myths, but have you ever watched a shimmering rainbow appear after a storm and wondered, *What's going on up there?*

Rainbows are created when sunlight and the conditions of the atmosphere are just right—and you're standing in just the right spot. For a rainbow to happen, water droplets must be floating in the air. And the sun has to be behind you—with no clouds in the way—for the rainbow to appear.

A rainbow occurs when sunlight shines on a floating water droplet. The light passes through the front wall of the droplet, then bounces off the back of the droplet and exits out the front again. As the light bounces inside the droplet, it separates into all the different wavelengths—or colors—of light. When the light reflects back toward you, you see all the colors of the rainbow.

TRY THIS!

MAKE YOUR OWN RAINBOW

- Get a glass and fill it about three-quarters full with water.
- Hold the glass of water above a white piece of paper.
- As sunlight passes through the glass of water, the light refracts (bends), forming a rainbow on the paper.
- Try holding the glass at varying distances from the paper to see how it changes your rainbow.

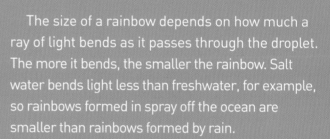

The size of a rainbow depends on how much a ray of light bends as it passes through the droplet. The more it bends, the smaller the rainbow. Salt water bends light less than freshwater, for example, so rainbows formed in spray off the ocean are smaller than rainbows formed by rain.

Rainbows don't actually exist in a specific spot in the sky. Instead, a rainbow is an optical illusion that depends on where the viewer is standing and where the sun is shining in the sky. This means that no one sees the same rainbow. For example, if you are looking at a rainbow, a person standing near the end of that rainbow will see another rainbow off in the distance. So you can never reach the end of a rainbow, no matter how hard you try!

Bet You Didn't Know!

Rainbows are actually full circles, but they look like arcs because the ground gets in the way. If you're ever in an airplane and are in just the right spot, you can see an entire circular rainbow. You can also see one by angling the spray from a hose just the right way!

CLOUDS: FLOATING WATER

It might seem impossible that water could float in the sky. But that's exactly what clouds are! Clouds are made of water droplets or ice crystals so small and light that they are able to stay suspended in the air.

There is water in the air around us at all times in the form of tiny gas particles called water vapor. They're so small that they're invisible. But there are also other tiny particles floating around in the air, such as salt and dust. These are called aerosols. Water vapor and aerosols constantly bump into each other. When the air is cool enough, some of the tiny particles of water vapor stick to the aerosols when they collide. This is condensation. Over time, the water droplets forming around the aerosols get larger and larger. They start sticking together, eventually forming clouds.

Different clouds have different names, depending on their shape and the height at which they form. Here are the 10 basic types of clouds.

HIGH CLOUDS:
ABOVE 20,000 FEET
(6,000 M)

MID-LEVEL CLOUDS:
6,500 – 20,000 FEET
(2,000 – 6,000 M)

LOW CLOUDS:
LESS THAN 6,500 FEET
(2,000 M)

CIRROSTRATUS

These thin white clouds cover the whole sky and are most often seen in winter.

CIRROCUMULUS

These thin clouds sometimes look like they're full of ripples.

CIRRUS

These clouds are made mostly of ice crystals. Wind currents twist and spread them, giving the clouds a wispy appearance.

ALTOSTRATUS

Ice crystals and water droplets mix together to form these clouds that usually blanket the whole sky.

ALTOCUMULUS

These clouds look like they're made of rows of fluffy ripples. They are made of liquid water, but they usually don't produce rain.

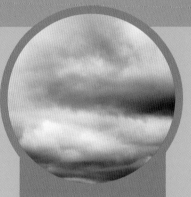

NIMBOSTRATUS

These dark gray clouds are so thick they can blot out the sun.

CUMULUS

These fluffy, white clouds are fun to watch. Their varying sizes and shapes can make them look like objects, people, or animals in the sky.

STRATOCUMULUS

These low, lumpy clouds are the most common clouds on Earth.

STRATUS

These thin, white, sheet-like clouds seldom produce rain or snow.

CUMULONIMBUS

When warm, wet air rises high into the sky on hot days, it can produce these clouds, which can grow into high towers.

SPOOKY SKYSCAPE

Lit by the moon, a castle stands in the distance. A low cloud hovers in front of it, so thick it's almost impossible to tell what lies beneath. Creepy! Fog can turn even the friendliest of fields into a scary scene. But fog is nothing more than a low-lying cloud.

Both clouds and fog form when water vapor condenses to form tiny droplets in the air. But whereas clouds can form at many different altitudes—some as high as 12 miles (19 km) up!—fog is a kind of low cloud that touches the ground. It forms when the air near the ground is cool enough to condense water vapor into liquid water or ice.

There are many different types of fog. One happens in swampy areas, when warm water vapor rises into cool air and condenses. Known as radiation fog, it can be hundreds of feet thick. Another type of fog forms when warm, moist air blows sideways—a phenomenon called advection—across a cold surface. This makes the air above the cool ground very moist, and as it cools, the water vapor condenses into a cloud.

It may be foggy in the morning, but fog usually disappears as the day warms up. Sunlight heats the air near the ground. As air warms, the dew point—or temperature at which condensation takes place—goes up. Water keeps evaporating from the ground, but now the water vapor has to float higher until it reaches an air temperature that matches the dew point. If the water vapor condenses high in the sky, the fog has been lifted.

VALLEY FOG

RAIN FOG

THE FOG FAMILY

Fog forms in a lot of different ways depending on the landscape, temperature, and amount of water in the air.

RADIATION FOG
When warm water vapor rises into cool air and condenses, it is known as radiation fog. The cloud can be hundreds of feet thick.

ADVECTION FOG
When warm, moist air blows sideways across a cold surface, it cools and its water vapor condenses into a cloud called advection fog. It often occurs when warm air passes over a snowy area.

VALLEY FOG
Downslope winds carry cool air from the mountains into a valley, cooling the warm, moist air between the slopes. The warm air condenses into low clouds that fill the valley.

FREEZING FOG
Sometimes a fog drops to temperatures below 32°F (0°C)—the freezing point—but without freezing. If that fog touches a solid surface, such as a tree, the supercooled water drops suddenly freeze. This makes an icy coating on anything the fog touches. Sometimes, ice fog forms when the temperature drops below 14°F (-10°C). The fog's water drops freeze while floating in the air.

RAIN FOG
Warm rain sometimes evaporates into water vapor before hitting the cool ground, which chills the incoming vapor. When that happens, the water vapor condenses into fog.

FREEZING FOG

You might think of California as a sunny place, but the coastal city of San Francisco is known for its summertime advection fog caused by warm air from the Pacific Ocean blowing over colder water along the coast. The phenomenon is so famous, it has a name: Karl the Fog.

Radiation fog sits along the water and surrounds the Kilchurn Castle in Scotland.

HAIL

Look out below! Hail is among the most dangerous types of precipitation. Hailstones can damage buildings, vehicles, and crops. In the 18th century, Europeans tried to prevent hail by firing cannons into clouds and ringing church bells. But nothing can stop this weather phenomenon. To this day, hail sometimes causes extreme damage to property.

Hail is formed in the cold upper regions of thunderstorm clouds when drops of water freeze together into chunks of ice called hailstones. Conditions have to be just right to create hailstones. They're made when a frozen droplet of water starts to fall toward Earth—but before it can get far, a strong updraft of wind pushes it back up into the cloud. There, it slams into liquid water droplets, which instantly freeze to the hailstone, making it bigger. If this process happens many times in just the right conditions, hailstones can grow to record-breaking sizes. Eventually, they get so big that gravity sends them plummeting toward the ground.

HISTORICAL HAILSTORM

In 1942, a British forest guard in Roopkund, India, made a startling discovery: a frozen lake full of skeletons. Experts dated the remains to around A.D. 850 and realized that everyone at "Skeleton Lake" had died from blows to the head and shoulders by blunt, round objects about the size of baseballs. The experts concluded the group had been caught in a deadly hailstorm!

BIGGEST HAILSTONE

On July 23, 2010, the world's largest recorded hailstone by diameter and weight fell in Vivian, South Dakota, U.S.A. Measuring a whopping eight inches (20 cm) across—nearly the size of a volleyball—it made a hole in the ground about a foot (0.3 m) wide when it landed.

MOST HAILSTORMS

Unless you like being pelted by hailstones, you might want to avoid visiting Kericho, Kenya, the place said to experience the most hail in the world: up to 50 days of hail each year. In 1965, it hailed there on 113 separate days!

COSTLIEST HAILSTORM

On April 14, 1999, hailstones up to 3.5 inches (8.9 cm) across fell in Sydney, Australia, for nearly an hour straight. They smashed up 20,000 structures and 40,000 vehicles, totaling $3 billion in modern U.S. dollars.

SHAPED BY WATER

It might seem impossible that the slow drip of rainwater or the flow of a river could carve away solid rock. But some of Earth's most spectacular spots were created exactly this way.

CAVE OF CRYSTALS, CHIHUAHUA, MEXICO

Situated 984 feet (300 m) below Earth's surface is a cave that looks like something from science fiction, with gigantic crystal pillars (some up to 36 feet (11 m) long!) sticking out of the floors, walls, and ceiling. How did they grow so big? When magma deep under the cave cooled, minerals in the water-filled cave dissolved and then began to form crystals. Over millions of years in the cave's wet, hot, humid conditions, the crystals grew to enormous size.

THE GRAND CANYON, ARIZONA, U.S.A.

At 277 miles (446 km) long, up to 18 miles (29 km) wide, and more than a mile (1,600 m) deep, the Grand Canyon is one of the world's most jaw-dropping natural landmarks. This enormous slash in Earth's surface was carved by water from the Colorado River flowing through the land beginning about six million years ago.

THE GREAT BLUE HOLE, BELIZE

Scuba divers flock to this huge underwater sinkhole—more than 984 feet (300 m) across and 410 feet (125 m) deep—to see the corals, giant groupers, and many species of sharks that visit Belize's Great Blue Hole. Long ago it was a cave system that collapsed when sea levels rose during the last ice age.

HA LONG BAY, VIETNAM

Ha Long Bay looks like the setting of a fairy tale, with turquoise water dotted with steep-sided limestone pillars. Ancient legends say dragons created these rocks to keep invaders out, but they were actually shaped by the rising and falling of the sea over 500 million years.

BRYCE CANYON NATIONAL PARK, UTAH, U.S.A.

According to legends of the Paiute Native Americans, the rock spires of Bryce Canyon were ancient beings that had been turned to stone. Called "hoodoos," some of these formations are taller than a 10-story building! They are created when melted snow seeps into vertical cracks, then freezes at night, expanding and prying them apart.

WAVE ROCK, AUSTRALIA

You might not be able to surf it, but it's surely one of Australia's most spectacular waves. Wave Rock is a 46-foot (14-m)-high, 361-foot (110-m)-long granite outcrop that was once buried by soil. Erosion wore the soil away from the top of the rock, allowing rainwater to run down the sides and dissolve it into its current shape.

Updrafts can reach speeds of more than 100 miles an hour (161 km/h).

THUNDERSTORMS

It's a hot summer night, and the rain pounds on your roof. Suddenly, a bright light flashes, followed by ... BOOM! Thunder roars across the sky.

What began as a rain cloud transformed into a thundercloud. Clouds form when moist air near the ground warms up and carries water vapor skyward. High up, the vapor cools and condenses into tiny water drops. They stick together to form a cloud. But there is something different about this cloud. When the air is very warm and moist, it moves upward, carrying heat energy from the land's surface into the upper levels of the atmosphere. The updraft of rising air grows into a very tall cloud—reaching up to several miles in height— to form a storm cell. Inside it, air moves up and down like it's on a roller coaster. At the top, the air cools to form water drops that turn into tiny pieces of ice. The cool air sinks back to the ground, creating a fast-moving downdraft. That downdraft can create a sudden downburst of heavy rain.

All the up-and-down movement of air churns the water droplets, bits of dust, and ice inside the cloud. They clump together and grow into larger raindrops and ice crystals. Soon they will be too heavy for the air currents to send upward again. But while they are still moving inside the cloud, the particles build up the positive and negative electrical charges that create lightning. (Find out more about lightning on the next page.)

Sometimes, thunderclouds can join together into multicells. The strongest type of thunderstorm comes from a supercell, which forms when the updraft spins inside the cell.

DEADLY DERECHOS

Sometimes, multiple thunderstorms can organize into a line that looks like a giant shelf in the sky. In this kind of storm, called a derecho—Spanish for "straight ahead"—winds blow at least 58 miles an hour (93 km/h) with gusts of more than 75 miles an hour (121 km/h). This giant wall of wind causes damage spanning more than 250 miles (402 km). Derechos can cause severe damage, knocking over trees, toppling power poles, and ripping off roofs.

INSIDE A THUNDERCLOUD

Ice, dust, and water particles become electrically charged and separate into positive and negative regions within the cloud.

Rising warm air creates an updraft that makes the cloud, or cell, grow tall.

Sinking cold air forms a downdraft that sends bursts of rain and wind to the ground.

ZAP! LIGHTNING

In 1752, Benjamin Franklin famously flew a kite with a key dangling from it during a thunderstorm to prove for the first time that lightning is a bolt of electricity. Today we know that lightning happens when electricity builds up inside a thundercloud. As lightweight particles, such as ice crystals, collide with larger, heavier particles, the lighter particles become positively charged while the heavier particles become negatively charged. Updrafts carry the lighter particles toward the top of the cloud, while heavier particles fall toward its base. Like a battery, the cloud now has a positive end and a negative end.

Eventually, the cloud builds up such a strong electric charge that energy blasts between its positive and negative areas. Most lightning, called intracloud lightning, happens this way. Only about 20 percent of lightning heads from the negatively charged cloud to positively charged objects on the ground—like trees, steeples, and buildings. This is called cloud-to-ground lightning, and it makes up most of the lightning you can see during a storm.

A typical lightning bolt begins when negative charges race downward from the bottom of a cloud toward the ground in a steplike pattern. At the same time, positive charge builds up on the ground beneath the cloud and is attracted to the negative energy at the bottom of the cloud. The ground's positive charge is concentrated in anything that stands up tall, like a tree. The positive charge from the ground connects with the negative charge from the clouds, creating a lightning strike. The flash that you see zips upward from the ground to the sky in about one-millionth of a second. A single lightning bolt has an incredible amount of energy—up to a billion joules. That's enough to toast 100,000 slices of bread! All that power means lightning sometimes sets fire to what it strikes.

Benjamin Franklin figured out that lightning is attracted to tall metal objects. He demonstrated that a metal lightning rod on the roof of a building can help divert a lightning bolt from striking it: Attaching a wire to the rod and leading the wire into the ground directs the incoming electricity down to the dirt. Damage managed!

BOOM BASICS

When a bolt of lightning flashes, it superheats the air around it—to 50,000°F (27,760°C), which is about four times as hot as the sun's outer layer. The hot air expands and then quickly slaps back together—just like when you clap your hands but much louder. BOOM!

Light travels much faster than sound, so you will see a flash of lightning before you hear the thunder that it creates. In fact, you can estimate how far away you are from where the lightning struck by counting. As soon as you see a flash of lightning, count "one Mississippi, two Mississippi ..." and stop when you hear thunder. For every five seconds, or five Mississippis, the lightning struck one mile (1.6 km) away.

Bet You Didn't Know!

Before scientists were able to decipher how this fantastic light show happened, ancient cultures created myths and legends to explain lightning. Long ago, the ancient Greeks thought the god Zeus could throw bolts of lightning at enemies. In Norse mythology, Thor wields a mighty hammer, creating lightning as he slays giants in the sky.

The chances of a person getting hit by lightning are about 1 in 5,000. But it's always best to take cover during a storm!

The record for
fastest rainfall is
1.23 inches (31.2 mm)
in one minute, set in
Unionville, Maryland,
in 1956.

FLOODS AND MUDSLIDES

It hasn't rained in months, and the ground is parched. Bushes and grasses are brown and dried, and the hillsides are brittle. Then rain begins to fall ... and keeps falling. That's a good thing, right? Not always.

Floods: When steady rain falls for days at a time, rivers swell and spill over their banks. Big rivers in the United States, such as the Mississippi, Missouri, and Ohio, are major transportation routes that are lined with a lot of cities. These cities have all experienced devastating floods from too much rain.

Ellicott City, Maryland, for example, experienced what's known as a 1-in-1,000-year rain in July 2016. In other words, the chances of that happening in any given year are about 1 in 1,000, according to the National Weather Service. Up to six inches (15 cm) of rain fell within two hours, causing the Patapsco River to rise by 13 feet (4 m), overflow, and completely flood the city.

Mudslides: Normally, when rain falls to the ground, the water soaks into the ground and trickles down among the roots of plants. But if there is an extreme amount of rain, or a sudden deluge of water as from a melting snowpack, the huge volume of water mixes with the soil, causing it to liquefy and move downhill. A big mudslide can make a whole mountainside wash away.

In August 2017, after a long dry season, heavy rains triggered a mudslide on the outskirts of Freetown, the capital of Sierra Leone in West Africa. The side of a small mountain in the town of Regent gave way during heavy rain, and a huge swath of soil slid down the slope like an avalanche of snow. As dirt flowed downhill, it swallowed up small houses, cars, trees, and anything else in its path. All told, 1,141 people were killed and more than 3,000 were left homeless.

RAISE THE GATES!

Flood gates protect cities from overflowing rivers in many parts of the United States. Louisville, Kentucky, has flood gates that channel overflowing water from the Ohio River into pumping stations. Meanwhile, tall concrete walls and mounds of soil shaped into levees complete a flood protection system designed to keep nearly 90,000 homes in the area safe.

Bet You Didn't Know!

Mudslides can move at speeds ranging from 30 miles an hour to 200 miles an hour (48 to 322 km/h) and move millions of tons of rock and soil.

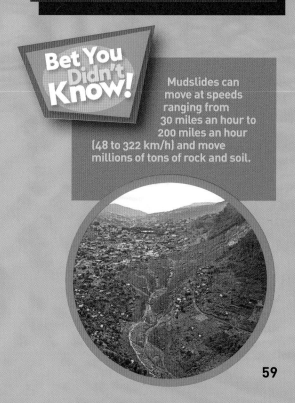

The World Meteorological Organization gives tropical storms names as a way to keep track of them. Different regions of the world have lists of names, each with a unique flavor. The lists for the South China Sea include names like Nock-ten and Lupit. Australia's lists include Iggy and Kirrily. The United States uses names like Fred and Vicky.

Palm trees in Miami, Florida, were blasted by winds of more than 100 miles an hour (161 km/h) during Hurricane Wilma in 2005.

HURRICANES

Hurricanes are the most violent storms on Earth. They are capable of producing extremely heavy rains that can cause serious flooding and violent winds. They form over the ocean, fueled by the warm seas of the tropics. If conditions are just right, the storm clouds will grow, become organized, and a low pressure center will form. Batten down the hatches as the system grows and spins faster and faster—a hurricane is born!

The Saffir-Simpson Hurricane Wind Scale classifies hurricanes as Category 1 through Category 5 based on their sustained wind speed. The faster the winds, the stronger the storm: Category 1 hurricanes have winds between 74 and 95 miles an hour (119 to 153 km/h); Category 5 hurricanes have the fastest sustained wind speed, clocking in at 157 miles an hour (252 km/h) and higher.

Even though hurricanes begin in the warm tropical regions, they can travel hundreds of miles at sea and move toward the coast. In October of 2012, Superstorm Sandy began as a tropical storm near Nicaragua, Central America. It grew into a Category 1 hurricane, with winds spanning out 485 miles (780 km) from its center. The storm traveled northward up the East Coast of the United States to New York—leaving a path of destruction in its wake—before heading inland toward the Great Lakes and into Canada. Because a hurricane gets weaker once it's over land, Sandy faded away in a couple of days.

When a hurricane hits land, it brings a lot of water with it. Heavy rain can cause flooding, but a bigger problem is a storm surge, or a sudden wave of seawater that the storm drags with it. When Superstorm Sandy reached land, it had weakened into what scientists call an extratropical cyclone. But it still caused extensive damage, partly because it hit during a full moon, which made high tides 20 percent higher than normal. The storm thrust a wall of water nearly 14 feet (4.3 m) high across the tip of New York City and the coast of New Jersey. Houses were destroyed, roads washed away, train tunnels and subways were flooded, and more than 100 people were killed. It can take cities and towns years to recover from a storm like that.

HURRICANE, TYPHOON, OR TROPICAL CYCLONE?

You might have heard all these terms used to describe huge spinning storms. But what's the difference? Hurricanes and typhoons are both considered tropical cyclones—a generic term that means a rotating storm system that is born over tropical waters. Once a tropical cyclone reaches wind speeds of 74 miles an hour (119 km/h) or higher, it can get a new name. In the North Atlantic, central North Pacific, and western North Pacific, it's called a hurricane. In the Northwest Pacific, it's a typhoon. And in the South Pacific and Indian Ocean, it keeps the name tropical cyclone.

Mangrove forests help protect coastal areas from hurricane storm surges by acting as a natural barrier.

CHAPTER 4
WINDY WEATHER

Most of the time, we barely notice the wind as it rustles the leaves above our heads or blows a stray piece of paper around the sidewalk. Other times, though, it's hard to ignore: The wind can turn our umbrellas inside out, lift roofs off buildings, and even blow cars around the highway.

Wind is the movement of air around Earth. It affects the weather of the entire planet, circulating air around the globe and blowing storms from place to place. Sometimes, winds can even swirl into one of Earth's most powerful weather events: tornadoes.

THE TRI-STATE TORNADO OF 1925

In 1887, the word "tornado" was banned from use by the U.S. Weather Bureau (now the National Weather Service) and remained that way for the next 38 years. The reasoning? Tornadoes were impossible to predict. Studying them was a waste of time, and using the word would just cause public panic. That argument was challenged when the deadliest twister in American history struck the midwestern U.S. on March 18, 1925.

At 1 p.m. on that day, a column of twisting air appeared near the town of Ellington, Missouri, killing a local farmer. Eighty-three minutes later, it had spun its way out of Missouri, killing between 11 and 13 people. And the twister was just getting started. At 2:26, the storm hit Gorham, Illinois. "The air was full of everything, boards, branches of trees, garments, pans, stoves, all churning around together," one survivor described of the scene. "I saw whole sides of houses rolling along near the ground." After destroying the town, the tornado moved on to the nearby city

The Tri-State Tornado left thousands of people without homes.

of Murphysboro. There it laid waste to a railroad repair yard, a school, and entire residential streets.

The tornado then went on to West Frankfort, Illinois, then crossed into Indiana, wiping out the towns of Griffin and Princeton. By the time its roughly 300-mile-an-hour (480-km/h) winds petered out, it had lasted 3.5 hours and traveled 219 miles (352 km). At a mile (1.6) km wide, the swirling column of air was so huge it was barely recognizable as a tornado. (In fact, some modern scientists think it could have been multiple tornadoes.) All told, there were 695 casualties, more than 2,000 people injured, and 15,000 homes demolished. Thousands were left without food,

Damage caused by the Tri-State Tornado

In 1925, 500 people per year were killed by tornadoes. Today, the number is 69.

and battled fires, looting, and theft in the wake of the disaster—one of the worst in U.S. history. It took some towns about 15 years to fully recover.

One positive legacy of the tragedy was the birth of modern tornado forecasting. Immediately after the disaster, local people formed networks that attempted to spot tornados and warn people in their path. Tornado deaths began to drop. But it wasn't until two decades after the tragedy that a more formal tornado warning system began to take shape.

On March 20, 1948, a tornado struck Tinker Air Force Base in Oklahoma City, Oklahoma, prompting a general on the base to ask two of his meteorologists to research how to predict future tornados. Just five days later, they reported that weather conditions looked extremely similar to those of March 20. They were right. A second tornado tore through Tinker, but because of the warning, planes were in their hangers and people had time to take cover. The damage was minimal. Soon after, the U.S. Weather Bureau (now known as the National Weather Service) ended the ban on the word "tornado," and experts have been working to provide warnings to people in the path of tornadoes ever since.

The fastest winds on Earth occur inside tornadoes, where wind speeds can reach more than 300 miles an hour (402 km/h).

THIS PAGE: These beachgoers in Key West, Florida, U.S.A., are depending on the wind to keep their kites aloft.

OPPOSITE: Wind farms, like this one in the Baltic Sea, harvest wind energy to generate electricity.

WHAT IS WIND?

All around Earth, the wind is always changing. Sometimes, it's nothing more than a light breeze. But other times, winds accelerate into a weather disaster. What's going on in the air around us?

We already know that wind is caused by changes in air pressure. Air molecules move from a region where they are tightly packed together (an area of high air pressure) to a region where there is more room for them to spread out (an area of low air pressure). That movement creates wind. Often, it's temperature that causes differences in air pressure across Earth's surface. Warm air rises, producing areas of high pressure, which makes cool air move in to replace the warm air with areas of low pressure.

Sea breezes and land breezes are two examples of everyday wind. Sea breezes occur when air over inland areas heats up during sunny afternoons. The air grows warm, causing it to rise. Cooler air from the ocean blows in to take its place. By late afternoon, sea breezes can blow dozens of miles inland. At night, inland temperatures can drop enough that the ocean becomes warmer than the land. That causes the effect to reverse, and winds called land breezes blow out toward the ocean.

Usually the areas of high and low pressure that forecasters show on a weather map are the kind that drive the wind we experience every day. Most of the time, there are only small differences between areas of high and low pressure, and the winds that result are spread out over large areas. We feel these kinds of winds as gentle breezes. But sometimes, there are big pressure differences between areas of high pressure and areas of low pressure. When that happens, air can move very quickly, creating high-speed winds.

WIND POWER

The wind is a constant source of energy moving around our planet. Humans have been tapping into this wind power for thousands of years: They've used it to push their sailing ships across oceans and to turn the blades of windmills to grind their grain.

Today, modern wind turbines capture the energy of the wind as it moves over the landscape. As the blades turn, they spin a shaft that leads to a generator, creating electricity. That electricity is used to power homes and businesses all over the world. Experts predict that by 2050, wind power could supply one-third of the planet's electricity.

GLOBAL WIND PATTERNS

Wind isn't just a force that cools you down or makes you pull your jacket tight around you to keep out the chill. Wind is constantly moving in patterns across the surface of Earth. These global wind patterns work to redistribute and circulate heat around the planet.

The paths that winds take around the planet are partly determined by something called the Coriolis force, an effect that occurs because Earth is a sphere that spins on an invisible axis. Earth is wider at the middle than it is at the top and bottom, so if you are standing on Earth's Equator, you will make a circuit of 25,000 miles (40,200 km) each day. But to a person standing anywhere that's not located on the Equator, the trip will be shorter. For example, if your friend were standing a foot (0.3 m) from the North or South Pole, he or she would travel only about six feet (1.8 m) that day! That means you and your friend would be moving at different speeds: You would be going almost 1,040 miles an hour (1,674 km/h), while your friend would be going just .00005 mile an hour (.00008 km/h).

The Coriolis effect exerts a strange influence on objects freely moving through Earth's atmosphere, such as wind: It shifts winds in the Northern Hemisphere to the right, and winds in the Southern Hemisphere to the left.

When the Coriolis effect combines with the uneven heating of Earth's surface, global wind patterns are created. There are three dominant wind patterns that generally blow in a steady direction across the planet: Tradewinds, Westerlies, and Polar Easterlies.

JET STREAMS

Jet streams are another kind of wind formed due to the rotation of the planet and the uneven heating of its surface. They are strong winds in the upper atmosphere that can blow as fast as 275 miles an hour (443 km/h). Airline pilots often fly near the bottom of the stratosphere, where jet streams blow. By getting a boost from a jet stream, pilots can save fuel and shorten flight times. There are two major kinds of jet streams: polar jet and subtropical jet.

POLAR JET STREAM

SUBTROPICAL JET STREAM

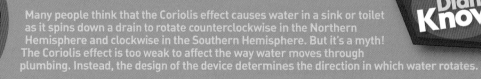

Bet You Didn't Know!

Many people think that the Coriolis effect causes water in a sink or toilet as it spins down a drain to rotate counterclockwise in the Northern Hemisphere and clockwise in the Southern Hemisphere. But it's a myth! The Coriolis effect is too weak to affect the way water moves through plumbing. Instead, the design of the device determines the direction in which water rotates.

GLOBAL WIND PATTERNS

As hot air rises from the tropics, it spreads north and south high above Earth's surface. At the mid-latitudes, about 30 degrees north and south of the Equator, it cools and begins to sink.

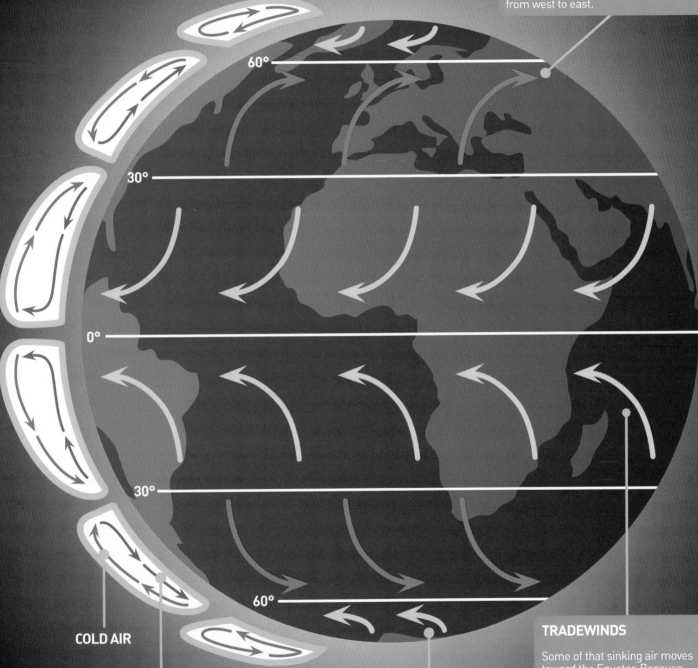

WESTERLIES

Some of that sinking air moves toward the poles. The Coriolis effect bends these westerlies the opposite direction from the way they were moving, blowing them from west to east.

60°

30°

0°

30°

60°

COLD AIR

WARM AIR

EASTERLIES

At latitudes higher than about 60 degrees, cold surface winds want to blow toward the warm Equator. But the Coriolis effect bends them just like the trade winds, making these polar easterlies blow from east to west.

TRADEWINDS

Some of that sinking air moves toward the Equator. Because of the Coriolis effect, these trade winds curve as they travel, blowing from the northeast in the Northern Hemisphere and the southeast in the Southern Hemisphere.

69

HIGHEST WIND SPEED

Tropical Cyclone Olivia above the Indian Ocean and heading toward Australia on April 10, 1996

CYCLONE OLIVIA'S PATH

Have you ever watched a strong gust of wind knock over a beach umbrella—or felt like one could knock *you* over? Then you might have wondered just how strong the wind can blow.

The fastest wind speed ever recorded on Earth, not including those inside tornadoes, occurred during a hurricane. On April 10, 1996, Tropical Cyclone Olivia slammed down on tiny Barrow Island, just off the coast of Western Australia. Within the cyclone was an individual mesovortex—a small swirling section of air that occurs within a storm. As it passed over the island, it produced five short bursts of extreme wind—the strongest of which reached 253 miles an hour (408 km/h). How fast is that? Compare it with winds in a severe thunderstorm, which typically gust at 50 to 65 miles an hour (80–105 km/h)! The wind burst was so extreme that experts were skeptical, and it wasn't until 2010 that the data was validated and the new record was official.

The previous world record had been held for more than 60 years by a wind that was recorded at the summit of Mount Washington, New Hampshire, U.S.A., on April 12, 1934. The blast, which traveled at 231 miles an hour (372 km/h), is still the fastest wind ever recorded in the Northern Hemisphere. Every year on April 12, the U.S. marks the event with Big Wind Day.

EXTREME SPEEDS

Tornadoes are famous for their high-speed winds. So why wasn't the record set by a tornado's swirling gusts? It's because tornadoes' wind speeds are really tough to measure directly—if scientists try, the extreme blasts will break their instruments! Meteorologists can only estimate tornado's wind speeds using Doppler radar, which works by bouncing microwaves off moving objects and analyzing how they bounce the signal back. If tornado wind speeds were considered, the record would be about 302 miles an hour (485 km/h)—the approximate wind speed during a tornado that swept Oklahoma, U.S.A., on May 3, 1999.

The slogan of Mount Washington, New Hampshire, is "Home of the World's Worst Weather."

Bet You Didn't Know!

Mount Washington's location makes it prime for wild weather. At 6,288 feet (1,917 m), it's the highest peak in the northeastern United States. It sits at the spot where storms originating in the Atlantic Ocean, the Gulf of Mexico, and the Pacific Northwest all cross—so Mount Washington is no stranger to strong weather. In fact, it's the site of a mountaintop weather station called the Mount Washington Observatory. Sounds like an extreme place to work!

ABOVE: Scientists use Doppler on Wheels radar trucks to collect data on tornadoes.

LEFT: The Mount Washington Observatory, completely covered in ice

A massive EF4 category tornado rampages toward a storm chaser's van near Manchester, South Dakota, U.S.A.

TORNADOES

Tornadoes most often form from a special type of thunderstorm called a supercell.

Supercells happen when there is a lot of energy and just the right wind conditions, causing moist air to rise 40,000 feet (12,192 m) or more into the troposphere. Then, that rising air starts to rotate. About 25 percent of the time, spinning air from that supercell twists itself down to the ground. A tornado is born. Exactly how tornadoes form from supercells is something scientists are still trying to figure out.

Tornadoes have been spotted on every continent except Antarctica. But they are most common by far in North America, where more than 1,000 touch down every year. And most of the time, they strike one particular area: a region of the Great Plains of the United States that covers Texas, Oklahoma, Kansas, and into Nebraska. This area, nicknamed Tornado Alley, has just the right conditions for twisters: Here, warm, moist air blowing in at the surface from the Gulf of Mexico meets cold, dry air aloft coming from the Rocky Mountains. When these cold and warm air masses collide, they create the right wind conditions (rotating updrafts and downdrafts) for the supercells that may spawn tornadoes.

In many countries, including the United States, Canada, and continental Europe, the strength of tornadoes is estimated by a rating system called the Enhanced Fujita scale, which classifies twisters from EF0 to EF5. An EF0 causes light damage such as topped trees and signs, while an EF5 causes incredible damage, such as houses being ripped off their foundations and demolished.

WHAT A WHIRLWIND!

Tornadoes are not the only swirling funnels in the sky. Dust devils materialize when one part of the ground, such as the dirt infield of a baseball diamond, heats up faster than the surrounding ground—perhaps a grassy outfield. Air warmed by the hot ground rises, creating a vertical column of warm rising air. If conditions are just right, the column will suck up more hot air from near the ground and grow stronger. These vortices of swirling air pick up dirt and debris as they go, which is how they get their name. On Earth, dust devils are usually small and harmless. But on the dusty surface of Mars, monster dust devils 10 times bigger than the biggest Earth tornado are commonplace.

DUST DEVIL

Swirling vortices of wind that occur over water are called waterspouts. Some, called fair weather waterspouts, develop just above the water's surface and then climb skyward. These are usually small and not dangerous. Other times, tornadoes form over water or move from land to water, causing tornadic waterspouts. Just like land tornadoes, they are associated with severe thunderstorms and can be very dangerous. Sometimes, they might even be able to pick up fish or frogs as they go, then rain them down somewhere else!

No matter the temperature outside, it's always cooler inside a tornado's funnel. That's because the vortex pulls in pockets of air, which expand as they move toward the center. As the air pressure drops, so does the temperature.

Bet You **Didn't** **Know!**

WATERSPOUT

HOW CAN A TORNADO PICK UP AND MOVE SOMETHING AS HUGE AS A HOUSE?

In 2014, a storm chaser following a tornado took some shocking video footage. In it, a home in Nebraska was lifted completely off its foundation, spun 180 degrees, then deposited right back where it came from—but facing the opposite way! Though the structure suffered severe damage, a father and his two young children survived in the basement while their house rotated above them.

Other tornadoes have been documented picking up big-rig trucks and tossing them around as if they were toys. They can sweep up trains and pick up cows. But how do they do it?

A tornado's shocking destructive force comes down to the speed of its winds, which can swirl at about 300 miles an hour (483 km/h) and fling debris. When these winds blow over a structure like a house, they exert uplift—the same force that

Destruction caused by the tornado that hit Pilger, Nebraska, U.S.A., on June 16, 2014

Even if it doesn't upend a home from its foundation, a strong tornado like this one can still inflict tremendous damage.

SPIN CYCLE

Sometimes, the destruction a tornado leaves behind is downright strange.

CORN HAIL: In 2015, an EF3 tornado near Pampa, Texas, lifted corn stalks so high that they became encased in ice, then fell as "corn hail."

BUGNADO: A dust devil over Vila Franca de Xira, Portugal, in 2014 not only pulled in dirt but also a swarm of insects. Viewers dubbed the 1,000-foot (305-m)-tall funnel a "bugnado."

CHAIR FORCE: A mile-wide (1.6-km) tornado that hit Joplin, Missouri, in 2011 picked up a kitchen chair at 200 miles an hour (322 km/h)—then hurled it at a store wall so hard the legs embedded into the stucco.

allows airplanes to fly. Wind enters the house, filling the structure with pressure as if it's inflating a balloon, and pushes up against the roof. The tornado's powerful suction and updraft draw objects up and inside, where the spinning vortex can hold them suspended in the air. As the tornado travels across the landscape, it can carry objects with it, which explains how they can end up in odd places.

In 1995, researchers at the University of Oklahoma wanted to find out how far a tornado could carry the things it picked up. So after a tornado, they asked people in the affected areas to send them objects with identifiable origins, such as checks, which include the name and address of the person who wrote them. They collected more than 1,000 objects and then mapped out how far they had traveled. While many flew an impressive 15 or 20 miles (24–32 km), a few traveled truly jaw-dropping distances—one even made it more than 150 miles (241 km) away!

People and rickshaws try to move through the flooded streets of the neighborhood of Paharganj in New Delhi, India, after a heavy monsoon rainfall.

MONSOONS

The word "monsoon" might bring to mind storms that drench the landscape with torrential rain. But that's not quite right. Monsoons aren't storms; they're seasonal shifts in a region's wind. Sometimes the shift may bring heavy rains, but other times it can cause dry spells.

Like all weather events, monsoons are caused by uneven heating of Earth's surface—in this case, the difference in temperature between a landmass and its nearest ocean. Most of the time during the summer, the land is warmer than the ocean. This makes air rise over the land, leaving a space that cooler air from the ocean blows in to fill. Because air from the ocean is full of moisture, this causes heavy rains over the land that can last for months at a time. This is called the summer monsoon.

The most famous summer monsoon occurs between April and September, when warm, moist air from the Indian Ocean blows toward India, Sri Lanka, Bangladesh, Myanmar, and other countries in the region. The summer monsoon causes these areas to have a humid climate and summers with torrential rainfalls.

Strong monsoons can be devastating, causing major flooding and fatalities. But many regions also depend on the summer monsoon. In India and Southeast Asia, farmers count on the monsoon's rains to fill wells and stores of underground water called aquifers. These water sources irrigate crops such as rice and tea throughout the year. Water collected during the summer monsoon season also powers hydroelectric plants that produce electricity for hospitals, schools, and businesses.

They aren't as well known as their rainy summertime cousins, but there are also winter monsoons. Winter monsoons are associated with dry wind, not rain. The best-known winter monsoons happen when air above Mongolia and northwestern China blows cool dry northeasterly winds over most of the Asian continent. The Himalayan mountains prevent much of the wind from reaching the coast, as well as places like southern India and Sri Lanka. That makes winter monsoons less powerful than summer monsoons.

THE NORTH AMERICAN MONSOON

Monsoons don't just happen in the tropics. There are monsoon winds in other parts of the world, including North America. Once a year—usually in the middle of summer—warm, moist air from the Gulf of California blows northeast, running into warm moist air blowing northwest from the Gulf of Mexico. The two winds collide over the Sierra Madre Occidental mountains in central Mexico, bringing a season of heavy rain, high winds, flash floods, hail, and lightning to the southwestern United States.

Bet You Didn't Know!

The North American monsoon can act like a natural firefighter, helping extinguish summer wildfires in the southwestern U.S., including Arizona, New Mexico, and Texas.

SHAPED BY WIND

It might seem impossible that winds could be powerful enough to wear away dirt and rock. But just give it a little time: Over millions of years, the wind has done just that, gradually scraping away at the earth to create some of the most incredible landscapes on the planet.

GOBLIN VALLEY STATE PARK, UTAH, U.S.A.

Despite its name, no ghoulish creatures live here—just rock sculptures so strange, you might find them haunting! This two-mile (3.2-km)-long valley is full of thousands of orange-brown, mushroom-shaped rock structures. They were created when the wind wore away sandy layers beneath the hard rock, leaving the rock structures balanced precariously on top.

SLOPE POINT, SOUTH ISLAND, NEW ZEALAND

South Island is constantly blasted by screaming, frigid winds that blow in from the South Pole, 2,980 miles (4,800 km) away. Aside from a few sheep and their farmers, almost nothing lives here. It's too bad, because the landscape is seriously stunning: Entire forests have been permanently bent by the gusts.

CERRO BLANCO, SECHURA DESERT, PERU

Dunes are mounds of sand that occur when the wind blows grains of sand into a sheltered area. Over time, those grains add up: Cerro Blano, in Peru, is one of the tallest dunes on the planet—perhaps the biggest in the world. At around 3,860 feet (1,176 m), it's taller than the world's tallest building, Burj Khalifa, in Dubai, United Arab Emirates.

SHILIN STONE FOREST, YUNNAN PROVINCE, CHINA

Okay, it wasn't just wind that shaped the jaw-dropping pillars of the Shilin Stone Forest—water helped! About 270 million years ago, this area was a shallow sea. As ancient shelled creatures lived and died, their shells were deposited in layers thousands of feet deep, which eventually hardened into two types of rock: limestone and dolomite. Later, geologic activity raised the seafloor, and wind and water eroded the rock, shaping it into giant vertical pillars.

DUNHUANG YARDANG NATIONAL GEOPARK, GANSU PROVINCE, CHINA

When the wind blows dust and sand over the land for a very long time, it can carve yardangs— sharp, irregular ridges in the land. That's what created this odd landscape in Gansu Province, China. If it looks alien to you, you're not far off: Yardangs have also been spotted on Mars!

CHAPTER 5
HOT WEATHER

It's the middle of summer. Your shirt sticks to your back; your shoes stick to the pavement. There's no breeze, and it's very still and quiet. Even the birds and insects seem to be snoozing the heat away. All you can think about is an icy Popsicle or a pool of water—anything to cool you down.

Sometimes, hot weather can veer from merely uncomfortable to downright dangerous. Heat waves can bake a landmass for months. Dust storms can cover an area in blowing sand in minutes. And droughts can dry it out for years. Here's how people and animals survive the world's hottest weather.

HEAT WAVE

In June, July, and August of 2003, Europe sweltered in a record-breaking heat wave. During that searing summer, temperatures rose up to 30 percent higher than their seasonal average in a huge area extending from northern Spain to the Czech Republic and from Germany to Italy. Many countries experienced their highest temperatures in recorded history, with some soaring above 107°F (41.5°C).

Many parts of the world routinely experience days hotter than that. But in those parts of Europe, days that hot are rare, and most people were unprepared: In France, for example, most people do not have air conditioners. As a result, more than 14,000 people died in France, and at least 30,000 died in all of Europe due to the heat wave. The heaviest toll on human life was on the very young, the chronically ill, and the elderly.

Besides the human lives lost, the 2003 heat wave had all kinds of effects across the continent. The Danube River in Serbia fell to its lowest level in a century.

A helicopter with a load of water flies over the deadly forest fires that swept across Portugal in 2003.

During the 2003 heat wave, Britain recorded its first ever temperature of more than 100°F (38.1°C), on August 10.

Bombs and tanks that had been submerged since World War II were exposed. Reservoirs and rivers that fed the public water supply dried up. The lack of rainfall created extremely dry conditions that fueled forest fires in many countries. In Portugal, about 830 square miles (215,000 ha) of forest were destroyed. And the heat caused snow and glaciers to melt away at record rates, creating flash floods in Switzerland.

Though heat waves don't get as much attention as other natural disasters, they are responsible for more deaths than floods, tornadoes, and hurricanes combined. And scientists calculate that climate change will likely increase the risk of extreme heat waves like the one that plagued Europe in 2003. The World Meteorological Organization estimates that it's likely the number of heat-related deaths on Earth will double in the next 20 years. What was an extreme occurrence in 2003 could be the norm by the 2040s.

To deal with the increased risk of heat waves, countries will have to come up with new methods for helping their citizens survive when temperatures rise. Since the 2003 heat wave, most European governments have developed action plans including warning systems and emergency measures for people who are most at risk.

TOP LEFT: A boy tries to cool off by running through a water sculpture in Barcelona, Spain, during the heat wave.

ABOVE: People often flock to beaches to get relief from record-breaking temperatures.

LEFT: A resident of the village of Sabugueiro, near Seia, central Portugal, tries to beat back the flames from one of the 2003 fires.

Extreme high temperatures can cause asphalt roads to melt.

Rows of corn in northeastern Louisiana shrivel beneath the sun during a July 2006 heat wave that hit the United States.

WHAT CAUSES HOT WEATHER?

Heat waves happen when air gets trapped above one spot on Earth's surface. Normally, air cycles around the globe—but during a heat wave, the air stays put, warming up more and more, just like the air inside an oven.

The 2003 European heat wave was caused by an anticyclone, an area of high atmospheric pressure that causes air to sink. Unlike normal rising air, the sinking air of an anticyclone doesn't form clouds, so they don't bring rain. Instead, they bring hot, dry weather. And when the ground becomes dry, it reduces evaporation, making things even drier.

When systems of high atmospheric pressure move into an area, air from the upper levels of our atmosphere is forced downward. That air becomes compressed, near Earth's surface, where the air pressure is high, causing its molecules to bump into each other at faster rates and its temperature to rise.

Sometimes a high-pressure system stalls out. When that happens, other systems can't move through. With no cloud cover to block it, sunlight can beat down on Earth's surface, making hot temperatures rise even higher. That's why heat waves commonly last for days or even months at a time. And the longer the weather system stays in place, the more the effects become amplified and the hotter the area becomes.

Sometimes, heat waves are intensified by the actions of jet streams, the high-speed winds that blow high in Earth's upper atmosphere, about five to nine miles (8 to 15 km) above the ground. Most of the time, jet streams blow weather from place to place around the globe. But when they are especially low-powered, weather—such as a heat wave—can stick around in one place for long periods of time.

HEAT WAVE SAFETY

- During heat waves, slow down and avoid strenuous activity.
- Wear lightweight, light-colored clothing.
- Drink lots of water, even when you're not thirsty. Eat foods high in water such as vegetables and fruits.
- Be very careful in parked cars, which can heat up extremely fast. Children and dogs should never be left alone in parked cars.
- Visit places with air-conditioning. Heat waves are a great time to check out your local library!

HIGHEST HEAT

Hottest Temperature

The highest temperature ever recorded was 134°F (56.7°C), at Furnace Creek in Death Valley, part of the Mojave Desert in California, U.S.A. Death Valley is famously the hottest place on Earth, as well as the driest place in North America. Summer temperatures there often exceed 120°F (49°C) in the shade. Because air warms as it sinks and compresses, one of the reasons Death Valley is so hot is its elevation: 190 feet (58 m) below sea level at Furnace Creek.

HEATING UP

Extreme heat waves, droughts, and wildfires seem to be becoming more common. Why? The past few years have been some of the hottest in Earth's recorded history. Eighteen of the 19 warmest years have all occurred since 2001, according to NASA. Scientists think climate change is the chief culprit behind the warming temperatures, and they predict that the hottest days are yet to come. If the warming trend continues, they say, by the 2050s there will be 20 record highs for every record low.

Longest Stretch of Days Above 100°F (37.8°C)

Going about your daily life gets a bit uncomfortable when temperatures climb above 100°F (37.8°C). Now imagine that they stay that way for 160 days—more than five months! That's exactly what happened in Marble Bar, Australia, from October 31, 1923, to April 7, 1924. Fortunately, the residents of Marble Bar were used to that kind of heat wave. The town is so far inland that cooling ocean breezes rarely reach it.

Greatest Temperature Increase in Two Minutes

At 7:30 on the morning of January 22, 1943, the temperature in Spearfish, South Dakota, U.S.A., was a frigid four degrees below zero (-20°C). But then, things started to heat up ... fast. By 7:32 a.m., the temperature had climbed to 45°F (7.2°C)—up 49 degrees (27°C) in just two minutes! Experts think the freaky fluctuation happened when cold and warm air fronts met suddenly.

Hottest Rain on Record

It's rare for rain to fall when temperatures rise above 100°F (37.8°C). That's because temperatures that high usually require a high-pressure system, which creates sinking air, instead of the rising air needed to form clouds. But the unexpected happened on August 13, 2012, in Needles, California, when the Southwest monsoon winds carried in moisture from the south and rain began falling at a temperature of 115°F (46.1°C).

Bet You Didn't Know!

Arica, Chile—a city in the Atacama Desert—went 14 years without a drop of rain. When the streak finally broke, in 2015, the desert exploded with colorful wildflowers!

TOO HOT:
STRANGE EFFECTS OF HEAT WAVES

These odd events actually happened during hot spells.

BUMPS AHEAD

In a scene that sounds like it came from an action movie, roads in Decatur, Georgia, U.S.A., suddenly buckled upward during extreme temperatures in April 2017. Buckling roads occur when a crack in the pavement lets in moisture, which then expands during hot temperatures and causes the road to warp.

DEADLY OCEAN

High temperatures don't just happen on land. In 2016, an underwater heat wave moved through the Pacific Ocean. The moving mass of hot water, nicknamed "the blob," caused the deaths of many marine creatures.

Russia

Alaska (U.S.)

Canada

The Blob

Japan

United States

PACIFIC OCEAN

Hawai'i (U.S.)

Mexico

Cuba

STRANGE SNACKS

During a European heat wave in the summer of 2018, animals at the La Palmyre Zoo in southwestern France were sweltering just like their human visitors. To keep the carnivores cool, zookeepers fed them blood-and-meat sorbets. This polar bear, at France's Mulhouse Zoological and Botanical Park, enjoyed a more traditional treat: frozen fruit.

HOT HANDS

Steering wheels can heat up to finger-searing temperatures when cars sit in the heat for hours on end. During a 2017 heat wave in Tucson, Arizona, U.S.A., some drivers resorted to slipping on oven mitts before putting their cars in drive—really!

NO FLY ZONE

One day in June 2017, Phoenix Sky Harbor International Airport, in Phoenix, Arizona, cancelled dozens of flights when the forecast predicted temperatures as high as 120°F (49°C). It might sound odd, but certain planes can't fly when temperatures rise too high. That's because as the temperature rises, the density of the air lowers. If the air density gets too low, there won't be enough lift generated on an aircraft's wings to get the plane airborne.

CAN YOU REALLY COOK AN EGG ON THE SIDEWALK?

If you've ever been outside on a really hot day, you might have heard somebody repeat the old saying, "It's so hot you could fry an egg on the sidewalk!" But is it actually possible?

First, some cooking science: Eggs are full of proteins, long chains of molecules that are all folded up. When the protein chains heat up, they unravel. Then, the loose ends of the chains become tangled up together until they form a web. That's what makes an egg firm when you cook it. And the temperature needed for that to happen is about 145°F (62.8°C) for egg white and 150°F (65.6°C) for egg yolk. (Much hotter than that, and the protein web will become extra tight, making your eggs rubbery.)

So, there's no reason you couldn't cook an egg on the sidewalk ... as long as the sidewalk gets hot enough. The problem is, it doesn't. Experts have found that the maximum temperature for a sidewalk is probably about 145°F (62.8°C). That should be hot enough to cook the egg white, if not the yolk. But when you crack an egg onto the sidewalk, the egg cools the sidewalk slightly. Concrete is not a very good conductor, or transmitter, of heat, so the temperature won't recover and the egg won't cook evenly.

However, there are other materials that could make better cooktops than the sidewalk. Dark objects absorb more light, so dark asphalt, such as on a road, would get hotter than concrete—maybe hot enough to cook an egg. Even better would be the hood of a car, since metal gets very hot and is a good conductor of heat. People have successfully cooked eggs on car hoods before—then they had a big mess to clean up, of course!

Bet You
Didn't
Know!

Every year on the Fourth of July, the city of Oatman, Arizona, holds a Solar Egg Frying Contest. Contestants get 15 minutes to cook a fried egg using the power of the sun—but they are allowed to get a boost from aids like mirrors and magnifying glasses.

TOO DRY: DROUGHT

Rain, rain, go away, come again another day. You've probably heard someone singing that tune during wet weather. But what happens when the rain goes away—and stays away?

In some places, it's normal to go for long periods without precipitation. The dry city of Los Angeles, California, for example, averages only 36 days a year with precipitation and typically goes months without a drop of rain, from late spring to early fall. The famously wet city of Seattle, Washington, U.S.A., in contrast, experiences an average of 152 rainy days a year. That's why drought means different things in different places. A drought isn't a certain time period that a place goes without rain. Instead, it's defined as a period of drier-than-normal conditions that causes water-related problems. Though droughts don't always involve hot weather, increased temperatures can make droughts more damaging.

If little or no precipitation falls, soils start to dry out and plants die. That can mean the crops that people depend on won't get harvested. If the drought continues for weeks or years, streams can run dry, and the water level in lakes, reservoirs, and wells can drop. This can create a shortage of drinking water and water for food crops. If water supply problems such as these occur, the dry period has become a drought.

Between October 2011 and September 2016, the U.S. state of California experienced its worst drought on record. Some scientists reported that it was the most extreme dry spell in the area since at least the year 800, judging by rings in the trunks of the region's trees, which vary in size depending on the rainfall that year. The drought raised prices on crops that require a lot of water, such as almonds. It also put wildlife at risk. Salmon, for example, depends on full rivers to migrate. And it made the region vulnerable to dangerous wildfires.

Scientists are concerned that in a warming world, higher temperatures could be making periods of drought worse. They predict that if temperatures continue to rise as they have been, there is a 99 percent chance that the U.S. Southwest will be struck by a megadrought, a period of extreme dryness lasting decades.

WHERE'S THE WATER?

The Aral Sea in Central Asia used to teem with fish and provide water for the crops of people in Uzbekistan and Kazakhstan. Two big rivers—the Syr Darya and the Amu Darya—flowed into this landlocked lake, which used to be the fourth largest in the world. Then in the 1960s, the Soviet Union's government built dams along the rivers. They used the water to create farmland by sending water to the nearby desert.

Since then, very little water has flowed into the Aral Sea, and it has dried up almost completely. Today, conservation efforts have built a new dam in the northern section. This is creating a small lake with a growing fish population. If the water is managed carefully, the Aral Sea may bounce back.

About 95 percent of the water that enters American homes goes down the drain.

THIS PAGE: The Big Salt Marsh at Quivira National Wildlife Refuge in south-central Kansas, U.S.A., completely dried up during a 2012 drought.

OPPOSITE: Camels cross the parched bed of the Aral Sea, located between the Central Asian countries of Kazakhstan in the north and Uzbekistan in the south.

In 2018, scientists discovered that dust storms blowing from the Sahara to the Americas could keep clouds from forming, possibly preventing hurricanes.

A haboob dust storm in Yuma, Arizona

DUST STORMS

WHOOSH! **You look up to witness a sight that looks more sci-fi than real life: A huge, dark wall is towering miles above the ground.** As you watch, you see that it's moving—fast. It swallows up entire towns as it crosses the landscape. When it reaches you, your surroundings are suddenly as dark as night. The wind screams in your ears, and sand and debris pelts you, choking your nose and mouth. It's one of weather science's strangest phenomena: a dust storm.

Dust storms happen most often over deserts and other regions where the soil is dry. Because of this, they often—but not always—occur in places that experience hot weather. Dust storms can be triggered by the event everyone in the dry area has been waiting for: rain. Hailstones and raindrops start falling—but it's so dry near the ground that they evaporate before they can touch down. That cools the air, and since the cold air is much denser than the air below, it falls quickly. It shoots toward the ground, then bounces back up, carrying dust with it. A dust storm is born. Dust storms can also happen when strong weather systems, producing strong winds, move across an arid region.

In the 1930s, the U.S. Southwest and central plains regions were struck by a nearly decade-long drought that dried up 100 million acres (40.5 million ha), creating the ideal conditions for dust storms. High winds and choking dust blew from Texas to Nebraska in an event called the Dust Bowl. People and livestock were killed, crops failed, and more than two million people fled their homes in search of livable conditions.

But dust storms aren't always bad. Scientists recently discovered that plumes of dust from the Sahara desert in Africa travel all the way across the Atlantic Ocean to South America's Amazon rainforest. Rainforests have poor soils, but the dust carries nutrients like iron and phosphorus that are key to plant growth. Dust storms allow one of Earth's most barren places to feed one of its most fertile areas.

HABOOBS

An Arabic word meaning "strong wind," haboob is a term that has long been used to refer to the infamous dust storms that commonly sweep across the Middle East and northern Africa. In 1971, a group of U.S. scientists borrowed the term to describe a severe dust storm in Arizona. The storm shared many of the characteristics of those from Sudan, including reaching an incredible height of 5,000 feet (1,500 m). The term has been used since then in the United States to describe these intense dust storms.

CHAPTER 6
COLD
WEATHER

When you open your curtains the morning after a snowfall, the scene outside is a winter wonderland. Everything is covered in a blanket of fluffy white, from buildings to cars to trees. You shove your feet into your snow boots and zip up your coat—it's time for a day of snow play! Sometimes, winter precipitation is beautiful and gentle. Other times, it brings wild weather, slamming cities with blizzards or coating them in a dangerous layer of ice. Cold weather events are some of the most extreme on Earth!

"SNOWMAGEDDON"

Students from Warrington, England, enjoy a snowball fight while visiting Washington, D.C., during Snowmageddon.

In the winter of 2010, the North Atlantic region of the United States was pummeled by record-breaking snowfall. Parking meters were buried. Schools were closed. To get out of their homes, some people had to tunnel out of their windows. And Niagara Falls partially froze! It was snow unlike many had ever seen before.

Between December 2009 and February 2010, three storms dumped an incredible 54.9 inches (139 cm) of snow on the area from Washington, D.C., to Baltimore, Maryland. That's nearly five feet (1.5 m)—taller than the average eight-year-old! It was the most snow that had fallen on the area since 1899. The snowstorm was so extreme that it earned the nickname "Snowmageddon."

Some people made the most of the event, using the roofs of their buried houses as makeshift sledding hills. But the severe snowstorm caused serious problems, too. The U.S. Postal Service stopped delivering for the first time in 30 years. Snow plows had trouble keeping up with the accumulating drifts. Planes were grounded and buses stopped service. Cars crashed on snowy highways. And hundreds of thousands of local residents lost electricity and heat for nearly a week.

In the aftermath of the storm, scientists set out to explain what set of weather circumstances had caused the massive snowfall. They determined that Snowmageddon came down to two major factors.

Other nicknames for Snowmageddon-type weather events have included "Snowpocalypse" and "Snowzilla."

TOP: A woman walks her dog past the U.S. Capitol during Snowmageddon.

ABOVE: A man digs out his car in Silver Spring, Maryland, U.S.A., on February 6, 2010.

The first was El Niño. A phase of climate pattern called the El Niño Southern Oscillation, El Niño is characterized by unusually warm sea surface temperatures of the tropical Pacific Ocean off the coast of South America. These increased temperatures heat the surrounding air, causing it to rise and condense into rain clouds in the tropics. This results in changes to jet streams, which can alter storm locations around the globe.

But El Niño doesn't always lead to snowstorms on the U.S. East Coast. For that to happen, there have to be colder temperatures—and that's where the second weather factor of Snowmageddon comes in: another climate pattern called the North Atlantic Oscillation, which controls the strength and direction of westerly winds. During the winter of 2009–2010, the North Atlantic Oscillation blew cold frigid wind from the Arctic down across the North Atlantic. Combine that influx of cold air with the storminess of El Niño, and you have a recipe for one monster snowstorm.

Bet You Didn't Know!

Many people believe that being out in cold weather can make you sick. But that's just a myth. What does make you sick are germs: The rhinoviruses that give you a cold are most common in the spring and fall, and the influenza viruses that give you the flu are at their peak in winter.

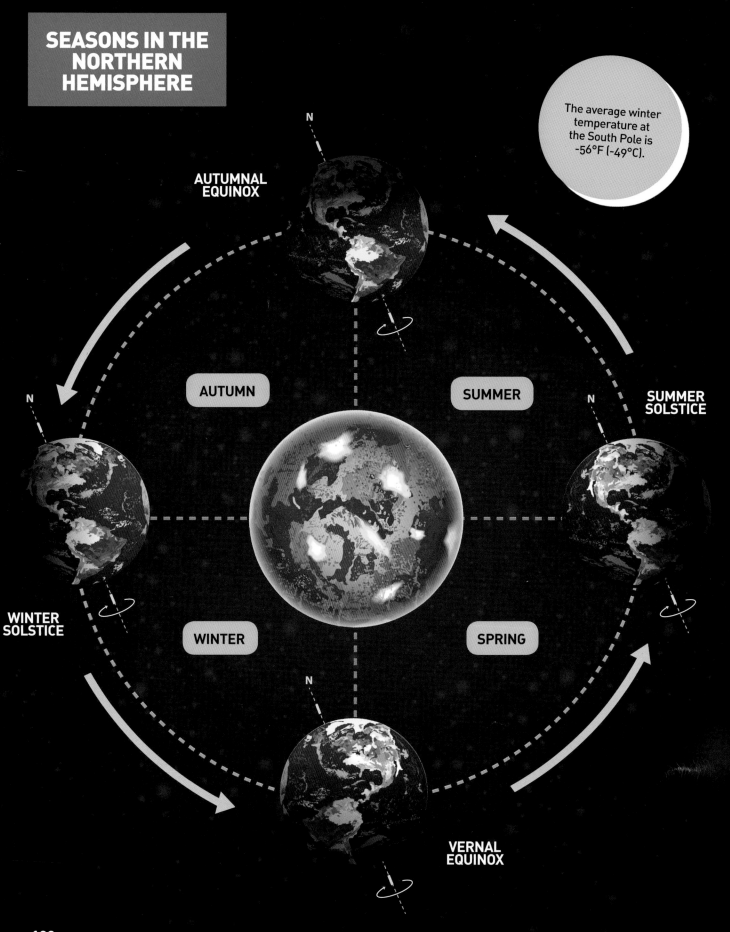

SEASONS IN THE NORTHERN HEMISPHERE

The average winter temperature at the South Pole is -56°F (-49°C).

N

AUTUMNAL EQUINOX

AUTUMN

SUMMER

SUMMER SOLSTICE

N

N

WINTER SOLSTICE

WINTER

SPRING

N

VERNAL EQUINOX

WHAT MAKES COLD WEATHER?

When the summer winds down and leaves start to change color, you might notice a nip in the air. After a season of heat, even 60°F (16°C) might feel cold! But in many areas, the thermometer will soon drop even lower: below 32°F (0°C)—the temperature at which water freezes into ice.

Winter weather happens in Earth's temperate zones (chapter 10) and at the poles (chapter nine). In the Southern Hemisphere, winter occurs when the South Pole is tipped away from the sun. People in the Northern Hemisphere welcome winter when the North Pole leans away from the sun. All of the coldest countries in the world are in the Northern Hemisphere, including Kazakhstan, Russia, Canada, the United States, Iceland, Finland, Estonia, and Mongolia.

Cold air at the North Pole must travel across the vast snow-covered lands of the Arctic then head south to reach the rest of the Northern Hemisphere. In the Southern Hemisphere, however, cold air from the Antarctic travels mostly across ocean water to reach the countries down under. Also, most of the landmasses in the Southern Hemisphere are already warmer than those in the north because they are closer to the Equator, which receives direct light from the sun all year.

Winter is a time when conditions are generally chilly. But sometimes, you step outside and WHOA!—things are extra cold. It's a cold snap! Periods of extreme cold, like other weather events, are caused by the movement of air masses. Generally, air masses have moderate temperatures. But every winter, giant cold Arctic air masses grow over northern Canada and Siberia. Their temperatures can reach as low as -80°F (-62°C)! When these air masses sweep southward, they can carry gusty winds and a sharp drop in temperature with them. Time to put on your gloves and scarf!

WARMING WORLD?

In recent years, many parts of the world have seen huge snow and ice storms. When you're buried under feet of snow, it may make you wonder—is the planet really warming up? Yes, say scientists. A cold snap in a particular area is a short-term weather event. When considering global patterns, it's the climate—the long-term weather average—that matters. Recent decades have been the warmest since at least around A.D. 1000, with the six warmest years on record all occurring since 2010. Short periods of cold—even if they break records—don't call the science of global warming into question.

WINTER WONDERLAND

Trees glisten as snowflakes gently float from the sky. A cluster of white ice crystals lands on your glove, and you can see the beautiful six-sided design of each snowflake.

Ice crystals begin to form when water vapor cools high in the sky to form tiny droplets of water in clouds. Two hydrogen (H) atoms and one oxygen (O) atom join together to create water molecules, or H_2O. When the cloud containing these water droplets rises higher into cooler layers of the atmosphere, or as cooler air moves in and lowers the temperature, the water droplets get cold enough to freeze into ice.

Clouds need to be cold for ice crystals to form—the process starts at around 14°F (-10°C). At temperatures that low or lower, ice crystals stick together, forming snowflakes. There can be as few as two or as many as 200 ice crystals in a single snowflake. When the hydrogen and oxygen that make up water freeze, they form patterns that give nearly all snowflakes six arms. Beyond that, snowflakes can come in all kinds of shapes and sizes. There are so many possible patterns that it's nearly impossible to find two snowflakes that look exactly alike (though contrary to popular belief, it is possible!).

Snowflakes can form if the cloud's temperature is low enough. But they can only reach the ground without melting if the temperature is below freezing the entire height of the atmosphere. It typically takes about an hour for a snowflake to fall from its cloud to the ground. Compare that to about three minutes for a raindrop!

SNOWFLAKE SHAPES

Sometimes, snow feels soft and fluffy when it lands on you; other times, it seems to sting your skin. It all depends on the shapes of the flakes. Scientists have classified more than 100 different types of snowflakes! They fall into four main categories.

PLATES
These are one of the most common types of snowflakes. They are light and flat, with six sides. They form under two conditions: when temperatures are just below freezing or lower than 5°F (-15°C).

COLUMNS
These delicate snowflakes aren't good for making snowballs, as their shape makes them less likely to stick together than other types.

NEEDLES
These long, thin snowflakes form in conditions of moderate humidity. They can pack together very tightly, making a snowfall of this type perfect for skiing or forming snowballs.

DENDRITES
These intricate, beautiful snowflakes need high humidity to form. Lots of moisture in the air allows the water vapor to condense rapidly, leading to the formation of complex branches. These snowflakes trap air, making for the fluffiest snow.

A two-foot square (0.2 sq m) by 10-inch (25-cm) deep block of snow holds about a million snowflakes.

THE COLDEST PLACE ON EARTH

Have you ever trudged through truly frigid weather that was so cold that your eyelashes started to freeze and the air seemed to burn your lungs as you breathed? If so, you might have wondered: *Just how cold is it possible for planet Earth to be?*

ABOVE: Winds from the East Antarctic Ice Sheet (the largest of Antarctica's ice sheets) create a moving carpet of ice crystals.

BELOW: A satellite view of Antarctica's Ferrar Glacier, a 35-mile (56-km) river of ice

In June 2018, the beginning of winter in the Southern Hemisphere, scientists found the answer. Previously, the record for coldest air temperature was at the Russian Vostok Station, near the South Pole. It was -128.6°F (-89.2°C)—air so cold that humans can't inhale it for more than a few breaths without blood vessels in their lungs bursting. In fact, scientists checking the temperature gauge had to wear special masks to warm the air they were breathing so it wouldn't kill them!

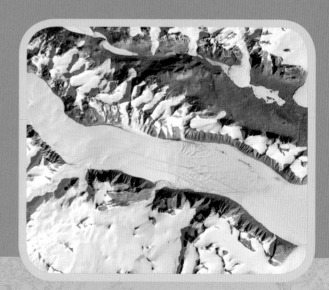

Russian researchers pose for a picture at the Vostok Station in Antarctica.

Bet You Didn't Know!

The coldest permanently inhabited place is the Siberian village of Oymyakon, Russia, where the temperature was recorded at -89.9°F (-67.7°C) in 1933. Brrr!

That's a truly frigid temperature. But researchers thought there could be somewhere on Earth that was colder still. Vostok Station is located on the East Antarctic Ice Sheet, which is slightly domed, with the middle higher than the edges. Vostok is near the top but not quite at the highest point. Scientists suspected that it might be even colder at the very peak of the ice sheet. There aren't any weather stations there, so they used satellites, which can read the temperature of the surface as they pass over from high in the sky.

When the researchers looked through the past several years of satellite measurements, they did indeed find a temperature that smashed the Vostok record: an eye-popping -144°F (-97.8°C)! It's the coldest temperature ever recorded on Earth—so cold, scientists say, that it's almost like conditions on another planet.

It takes a very special set of circumstances to create temperatures that low. It has to be winter, when the sun never rises at the South Pole. The air has to be perfectly still, and the sky has to be totally clear with no clouds at all. That's because even something as cold as ice gives off a tiny bit of heat—which is normally captured by water vapor in the atmosphere and reflected back to Earth, trapping the warmth near the surface. But when the weather is totally dry and there are no clouds, that little amount of heat emitted by the ice is free to escape all the way to space.

These dry conditions are not only good for creating record-breaking low temperatures: They are also ideal for getting an unobstructed view into space. That's why after Earth's coldest spot was pinpointed, another team of scientists placed a telescope nearby!

HOW DOES COLD WEATHER PRESERVE MUMMIES?

Ötzi the Iceman mummy on display at the South Tyrol Museum of Archaeology in Bolzano, Italy

Bet You Didn't Know!

Ötzi had 61 tattoos. Because the markings were located on areas of the body that are places where people today receive acupuncture treatments—including ankles, wrists, knees, and lower back—some scientists think they may have been an early form of pain treatment.

In 1991, a pair of hikers exploring the Alps mountain range on the border of Austria and Italy came across something shocking—a body sticking out of the ice. At first, they thought the remains belonged to a modern hiker who had lost his way. But when archaeologists examined the body, it was revealed that he had been lying there for a very long time: Scientific dating determined he had died 5,300 years ago!

The prehistoric body was nicknamed Ötzi the Iceman. He was so perfectly preserved that scientists were able to see the tattoos that covered his skin, examine the tools he was carrying, and even figure out what he had eaten for his last meal!

When Ötzi collapsed on the Alpine hillside more than 5,000 years ago, his body landed in a small depression surrounded by large rocks. Experts believe the hollow likely filled with snow immediately, covering the body and artifacts. Because of this, Ötzi was not discovered by thieves, who might have stolen his food and weapons, or predators, which would have destroyed his body.

Even if they're not discovered by hungry animals, bodies normally begin to deteriorate within a few minutes after death. Tissues and organs break down, beginning with the liver and brain. As cells die, bacteria that live in and on the body start to digest them. Decomposing tissue emits noxious-smelling gases that attract insects, which come to make a gruesome meal out of the remains.

But when a person dies in supercold conditions, like Ötzi did, the decomposition process is disrupted. The cells freeze, which prevents them from decaying. Bacteria and insects can't survive in extremely low temperatures, so they aren't there to break the body down. It's rare, but if the body stays cold, as Ötzi's did, it can remain intact for thousands of years.

For scientists, discovering Ötzi was almost like meeting a prehistoric person who had time-traveled to the present. They analyzed his tools, which included a copper axe, a dagger, and two arrowheads. They discovered that he had carried a primitive medical kit—birch fungus that naturally kills bacteria and treats inflammation. And they found that he might have been on the run at the time of his death: He had deep cuts on his hand and an arrowhead lodged in his shoulder, and he had received a fatal blow to the back of his head.

Despite decades of analysis, the Iceman is still revealing secrets: Recently, researchers reported that the Iceman has at least 19 relatives still living in Austria!

A memorial to Ötzi stands near the Tisenjoch mountain pass in the Alps, not far from the spot where he was discovered.

TRY THIS!

FROZEN BUBBLES

You don't need to wait until summer vacation to enjoy blowing bubbles! The next time it's supercold outside (below freezing) but not too windy, bundle up and ask a grown-up for permission to head out with a bottle of bubble solution. Blow a bubble and catch it on the wand that comes with the bottle. How long before it freezes? What about when you blow the bubbles up into the air? How long before they freeze? Check out the patterns on the frozen bubbles. What happens when you touch them?

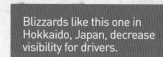

Blizzards like this one in Hokkaido, Japan, decrease visibility for drivers.

BLIZZARDS

Snowfall so thick it blots out the sky. Gusting winds. Cars and houses encased in ice. This is one extreme snowstorm. It's a blizzard!

People often use the term "blizzard" anytime a big winter storm blows in. But a blizzard is actually a particular type of storm, one with a high amount of falling snow and winds that exceed 35 miles an hour (56 km/h), creating visibility of less than one-quarter of a mile (0.4 km) for at least three hours.

Blizzard conditions often develop on the northwest side of a strong storm system. The air inside the storm is a lower pressure than the air to the west, creating an extreme pressure difference. That causes very strong winds, which blow snow as it falls from the sky and push snow that has collected on the ground into big mounds called drifts. Massive snowdrifts can bury cars and trains, and trap people inside their homes.

The term "blizzard" originated in the central United States, where it first appeared in an Iowa newspaper to describe a severe snowstorm in the 1970s. In the U.S., blizzards are most common in the upper Midwest and Great Plains states. In the Midwest, blizzard conditions sometimes come with extreme wind chills below -60°F (-51.1°C)! But they can happen anywhere in the world that strong snowstorms hit—so if your local meteorologist issues a blizzard warning, make sure to have your snow shovel handy!

Snow is white because incoming light reflects, or bounces off, all of the ice crystals in snowflakes.

THE LAKE EFFECT

The city of Buffalo, New York, U.S.A., sits at the eastern edge of Lake Erie. It is known for its "lake-effect" snow, which has been known to dump 40 inches (102 cm) of snow in a single storm. In fact, in 2010 Buffalo saw that much snow ... but only in the southern half of the city! About 10 miles (16 km) away, the northern half of the city saw almost no snow at all.

As cold Canadian air blows eastward across Lake Erie, it picks up moist warm air from the lake's surface. The moisture cools to form ice crystals in the moving clouds that form a narrow band. All that water often doesn't get very far: When the clouds make landfall, they drop a heavy load of snow in a small area. Unless the lake freezes over, it is a constant supply of warm, moist air.

Workers clear snow in front of a building in Buffalo, New York, after a powerful 2014 storm.

ICE STORMS

One dark and stormy night, you fall asleep to the sound of rain on the roof and wake up to a scene straight out of a movie. Trees bend to the ground, encased in ice. Your mailbox is frozen shut inside a capsule of thick ice. The sidewalk is the narrowest ice rink you've ever seen. It's an ice storm, one of nature's most beautiful— and dangerous— weather phenomena.

Ice storms occur because of freezing rain, which forms as a liquid in a relatively warm layer of air. But then, on their way to the ground, the drops fall through a shallow layer of below-freezing air just above Earth's surface. The temperature of the drops plummets, so when they strike the ground, trees, cars, or any other surface, the drops instantly freeze into ice.

As the freezing rain continues, ice accumulates in a coating known as glaze. It covers every surface in a dazzling sheen, but glaze is also highly dangerous. Just a half-inch (1.3 cm) of ice can add about 500 pounds (226 kg) to power lines, causing them to droop dangerously low. If they break, they cut heat and power to homes and businesses that are already battling cold conditions. The ice can increase the weight of tree branches by up to 30 times their weight, sometimes bringing them crashing to the ground. Even small amounts of ice can make sidewalks, roads, and bridges very slippery and dangerous to drivers and pedestrians.

ICE STORM OF THE CENTURY

It was January 1998. A tropical storm near Texas sent warm air northward. Cold Arctic air blew south. The two air masses bumped together near the Great Lakes, creating a week of ice storms in New England and Canada now known as the North American Ice Storm of 1998. Freezing rain blasted cold surfaces with at least three inches (7.5 cm) of ice that was so heavy it toppled trees and power lines. Millions of homes, farms, and businesses lost heat and power for weeks. Almost a thousand people got hurt, and around 40 died. It cost more than $3 billion to repair the damage.

Scientists simulate ice storms to figure out where and how often they may strike in the future.

Bet You Didn't Know!

The Inupiaq people have more than 100 words for sea ice, based on the many different kinds that can be found in their Alaskan home. Scattered pack ice, for example, is *tamalaaniqtuaq*, while floating pack ice is *sigu*. Large pieces of dark ice are called *taagluk*, and large floes are known as *puktaaq*.

THIS PAGE: Freezing rain accumulates on tree branches and forms a glaze that becomes so heavy the limbs can break off and bring down power lines.

OPPOSITE: Ice storms can damage utility poles, like this one in Saint-Jean-sur-Richelieu, Quebec.

Scientists are concerned that ancient microbes trapped in very old ice could be released as it thaws, causing disease outbreaks.

An elephant walks through the plains of eastern Africa with a snow-covered Mount Kilimanjaro in the background.

ANCIENT ICE

Bits of dust and air bubbles stored inside ice that has been frozen for a long, long time can reveal details about Earth's ancient history. To retrieve samples of the oldest ice yet discovered on Earth (about 2.7 million years old!), scientists in Antarctica drilled into the ice and extracted a sample, called a core, from deep down.

But Earth's ice doesn't just hold a history lesson—it's necessary to the survival of the planet's living things. About 69 percent of all the world's freshwater is frozen in the polar ice caps and glaciers. (The rest is in freshwater lakes, rivers, streams, and groundwater.) Glaciers are huge masses of ice that move very slowly over land; today, glaciers cover about 10 percent of the planet. Around 18,000 years ago, glaciers covered about one-third of the planet, including much of North America and Europe. As they moved and spread, they dramatically altered the landscape, plowing down forests, hills, and mountainsides, and carving deep valleys, such as what today is Yosemite National Park.

Normally, glaciers grow in size in the winter: As snow falls, it presses down on the layers of ice underneath, which slowly form a thickened mass of ice. And in the summer, glaciers melt a bit, filling rivers and streams that people, plants, and animals rely on for water. But all around Earth, glaciers are melting much faster than they have in the past, due to warming caused by climate change.

Even though the water in ice caps and glaciers stays mostly frozen, it has a big impact on Earth's weather. Its bright white color reflects away the sun's heat, and so it affects global weather patterns. Huge amounts of ice also lower air temperatures and contribute to dramatic winds.

Bet You Didn't Know!

Another type of ice is permafrost, ground that stays frozen for two or more years in a row. It's made up of rock, soil, other particles, and ice that binds them together. Some of Earth's permafrost has been frozen for hundreds of thousands of years and can be more than 3,300 feet (1,000 m) thick. Like glaciers, permafrost in many areas is now melting. When permafrost thaws, it releases carbon dioxide and methane into the atmosphere—gases that act like a blanket around Earth, heating up the planet even more.

THE CHILLY CRYOSPHERE

All together, the layers of ice that cover different parts of the planet are called the cryosphere.

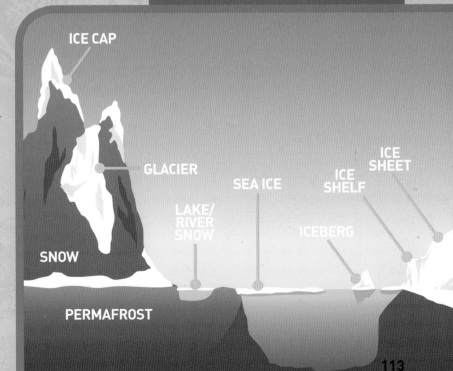

ICE CAP

GLACIER

SEA ICE

ICE SHELF

ICE SHEET

LAKE/RIVER SNOW

ICEBERG

SNOW

PERMAFROST

113

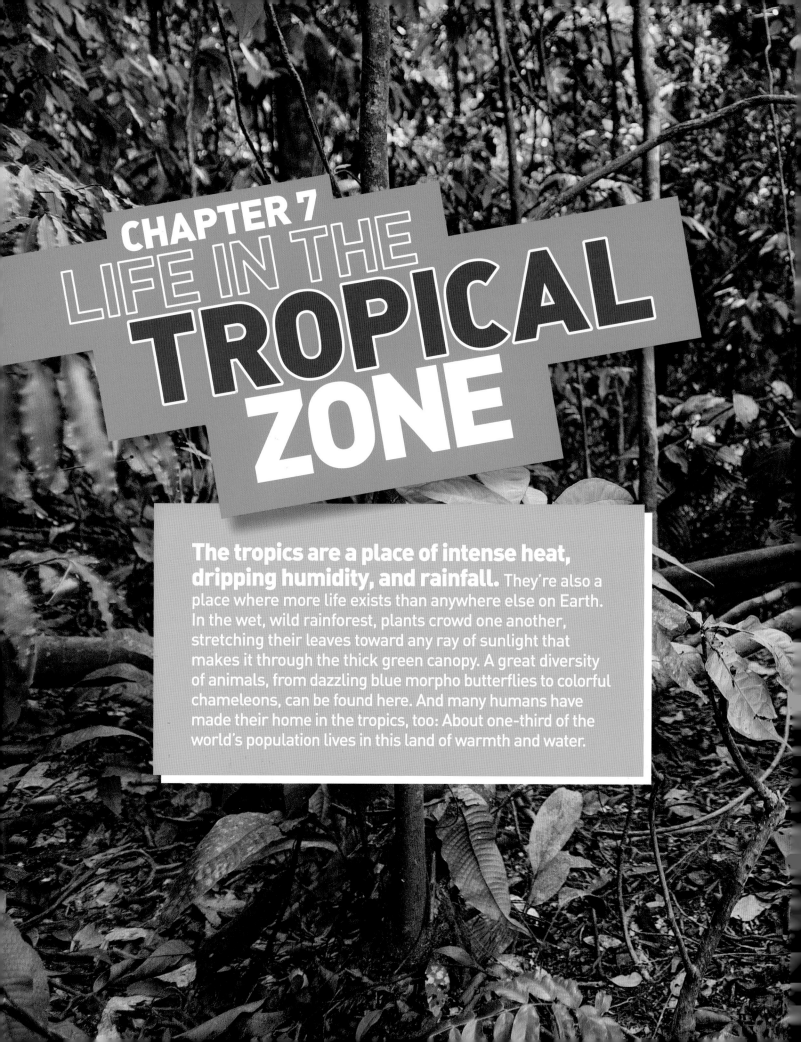

CHAPTER 7
LIFE IN THE TROPICAL ZONE

The tropics are a place of intense heat, dripping humidity, and rainfall. They're also a place where more life exists than anywhere else on Earth. In the wet, wild rainforest, plants crowd one another, stretching their leaves toward any ray of sunlight that makes it through the thick green canopy. A great diversity of animals, from dazzling blue morpho butterflies to colorful chameleons, can be found here. And many humans have made their home in the tropics, too: About one-third of the world's population lives in this land of warmth and water.

Sumatran orangutans sit in a forest clearing in Gunung Leuser National Park, Sumatra, Indonesia.

The tropics extend around the globe on both sides of the Equator, between the latitudes of 23.5 degrees north and 23.5 degrees south.

A woman rows the Rio Negro in South America in the rain.

CLIMATE IN THE TROPICS

Tropical rainforests are found near Earth's Equator, where the sun's light hits the planet most directly. That makes the climate warm all year-round, with average temperatures between 77 and 82°F (25 and 28°C).

The tropics are also known for rainy weather. High temperatures make water—especially water from nearby warm oceans—rise into the air in mass quantities. All that water in the air makes the climate very humid, and that humidity means a lot of rain. Some regions, like parts of the Amazon Basin in South America, get drenched in nearly 12 feet (4 m) of rain per year.

In some areas of the tropics, the weather is basically the same every day. You can expect near-daily showers, warm nights, and hot days. In other parts, there are just two seasons: a dry season and a rainy season. For half the year, trade winds blow in seasonal rains, called monsoons, drenching the land below. Then, the winds reverse direction, making the weather dry for the other half of the year.

Sometimes, large, intense, rotating storms form over warm tropical oceans. These tropical cyclones (also called typhoons or hurricanes) pull energy from the warm ocean waters and generate winds that can blow more than 74 miles an hour (119 km/h)—faster than a car on the highway! When cyclones hit land, they can cause serious harm to coastal communities.

FEELING THE HEAT

Tropical rainforests are a balancing force against the effects of climate change. That's because their dense plant life absorbs carbon dioxide from the air, sucking it out of the atmosphere and socking it away in their leaves, stems, and trunks.

But recent studies have shown that because huge portions of the rainforest are now being cut down, the effect has reversed: Instead of removing carbon *from* the atmosphere, rainforests are now *adding* more. Scientists estimate that rainforests currently release about 425 million tons (385.5 t) of CO_2 every year—more than what's emitted by all cars and trucks in the U.S. combined. The good news, though, is that the problem is reversible. If nations limit deforestation, rainforests will begin soaking up carbon once more.

LOST IN THE AMAZON

Yossi Ghinsberg was 22 years old when he became entranced by the idea of visiting the rainforest. In 1981, the Israeli adventurer traveled to La Paz, Bolivia, where he met an Austrian man who claimed to be an expert guide. The man told Ghinsberg he was planning an expedition to search for gold in a remote village. Little did Ghinsberg know he wouldn't find riches—he would barely make it back alive.

Ghinsberg was heading into one of the most extreme climates on Earth. The Amazon rainforest is hot, reaching more than 90°F (33°C), with nearly 100 percent humidity. Every year, torrential rains fall, releasing massive amounts of precipitation in some places and setting off huge floods.

Along with two other young travelers, Ghinsberg and his guide set off into the wilderness. But only two weeks into the trip, their meager supplies of rice and beans ran low. Exhausted from long days of hiking with little to eat, tensions rose. The group decided to split up: Ghinsberg and a young American photographer would build a raft and sail down the Beni River. The guide and the other traveler decided to continue on foot. They were never seen or heard from again.

Ghinsberg and his companion met disaster almost immediately: The river swept them crashing into a rock. The photographer was knocked off the raft and swam to shore, but Ghinsberg was left clinging to the remains of the raft. After a 20-minute ride through violent rapids, he was washed ashore. He had no food and no idea how to find his way back to civilization. Ghinsberg trekked through the jungle day after day after day. The damp forest floor soaked his feet, and the walking rubbed his skin away until his feet were raw and infected. He foraged for fruit and for eggs from jungle chickens, but he began to slowly starve to death. At one point, he woke up with a jaguar staring him in the face, ready to pounce. At another, he nearly died in a sudden flood—a common event during the rainforest's wet season.

After 20 days of battling the hot, humid conditions, something miraculous happened. Ghinsberg spotted a boat—and in it was his American companion who had been washed off the raft weeks prior. The American had found his way to a settlement and then gone back with a local to look for his friend. They were just about to give up the search when they spotted Ghinsberg, disheveled, 35 pounds (16 kg) lighter, and nearly unrecognizable.

Ghinsberg had fortune on his side. He battled the Amazon's oppressive heat and humidity, its extreme terrain, and its dangerous creatures—and he lived to tell the tale.

OPPOSITE: Yossi Ghinsberg before starting on his trip
TOP: Yossi (right) and friends after the trip
ABOVE: Yossi after he was found

PEOPLE IN THE TROPICS

Adventurers have lost their lives trying to find their way through the rainforest. But other people have been making this climate zone their home for thousands of years. How do humans survive in the hot, humid conditions of the tropics?

The combination of warmth and moisture helps many plants and animals thrive. But that doesn't mean the rainforest is an easy place for people to live. Plants grow so rapidly that they drain nutrients from the forest floor, and the nutrients that do make it into the soil are leached out by the constant rainfall. That makes farming very difficult.

Humans who make their home here, such as the indigenous Yanomami people (pictured), have traditionally been hunter-gatherers. They collect nuts and fruits when they are in season. They eat insects and hunt animals, such as wild pigs. To get enough food to survive, they have to travel through thick vegetation and avoid the rainforest's many dangerous plants and animals, from the aggressive Brazilian wandering spider to the deadly pit viper. Living in such a hot, humid, and wet climate has shaped the way people build their homes, what they eat—and even how their bodies work!

AMAZING ADAPTATIONS

People have been living in the rainforest for at least 20,000 years. Over that time, they have adapted, or changed gradually over many generations, to better fit their environment. Many people native to the rainforest are small in stature. Experts believe small bodies may help them in a number of ways: They require less food, which makes it easier to survive in a place where food can be scarce. They create less heat, making them less likely to overheat in their warm climate. And they are more agile, making it easier to climb trees and move through the dense forest.

The hammock was invented by the people of Central and South America to keep them off the ground, and away from the snakes and spiders that thrive in the warm, wet rainforest.

The Kayapo people are one of the groups of indigenous peoples of Brazil who live along the Xingu River and its tributaries.

121

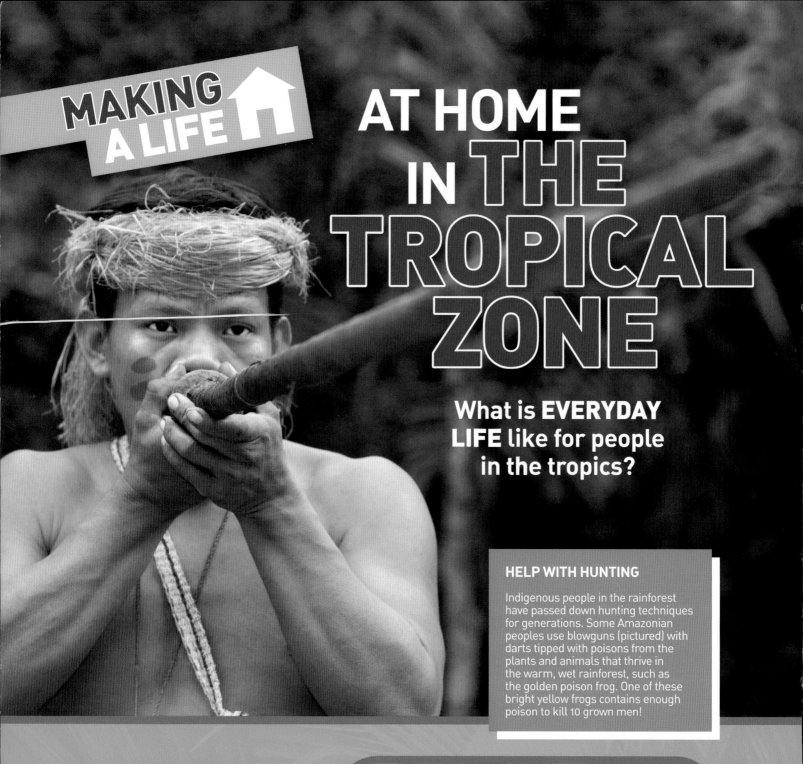

AT HOME IN THE TROPICAL ZONE

What is EVERYDAY LIFE like for people in the tropics?

HELP WITH HUNTING

Indigenous people in the rainforest have passed down hunting techniques for generations. Some Amazonian peoples use blowguns (pictured) with darts tipped with poisons from the plants and animals that thrive in the warm, wet rainforest, such as the golden poison frog. One of these bright yellow frogs contains enough poison to kill 10 grown men!

SUSTAINABLE FARMING

Though they depend on the forest for hunting and gathering, many indigenous people in the tropics also grow some of their food, like bananas and rice. Farming is difficult in the poor soil of the rainforest, so they use a technique called shifting cultivation: clearing a plot of land, planting, and then moving their gardens to a new plot every few years. This sustainable way of farming allows the rainforest to grow back.

HOMES ON RAFTS

Every year, about 97,000 square miles (250,000 sq km) of the Amazon rainforest are covered by water when rain causes the mighty Amazon to overflow its banks. Many homes there, such as this one in Brazil, are built on rafts so that the people can ride out the changing water levels.

HEALING PLANTS

The people of the tropics have been treating wounds and illness with plants from the rainforest for thousands of years. Today, some scientists are tapping the knowledge of tribal healers to help them find substances they can make into new medicines. Already, medicines to treat malaria and cancer have been derived from rainforest plants.

RIVERS AS ROADS

Because the thick jungle is tough to navigate, many people of the tropics use the rivers as their roads when they need to travel long distances. Indigenous people in tropical regions have traditionally made canoes, such as the one above, by hollowing out trees.

Bet You Didn't Know!

Mosquitos thrive in the humid climate of the tropics. To protect themselves from diseases these insects carry, such as malaria, the Sataré Maué indigenous people of Brazil endure the painful bites of the tocandira ant, which provides a natural defense against mosquito-borne illnesses.

123

PLANTS AND ANIMALS OF THE TROPICS

Living things thrive with the rainforest's nearly constant supply of water: More kinds of plants and animals live in the tropics than in any other place on Earth. Some estimates say there are as many as 30 million plant and animal species in tropical rainforests—that's more than half of all plant and animal species in the world!

Not much light makes it through the tall, thick canopy all the way to the forest floor. But rainforest plants have adapted to surviving in a place where rain is constant and competition for light is fierce. Many plants have elongated leaves called drip tips that help water run off instead of collecting on the leaf, where it could cause fungus and bacteria to grow. Some plants, like liana vines, hitch a ride to the light on other trees, climbing up their trunks high into the tree canopy. Some plants, called epiphytes, don't root in the ground at all—these orchids, some ferns, and relatives live directly on tree trunks and branches. They get all the nutrients they need from rain and air.

These plants provide shelter and a source of food for all kinds of rainforest animals, from crawling insects to swinging monkeys. There are so many animals competing to survive here that many have become specialists, meaning they are only adapted to live in one particular area. Bornean orangutans, for example, live only on the Southeast Asian island of Borneo, where they are found only in lowland forests, rarely venturing up higher than 1,640 feet (500 m) in elevation.

TOP TO BOTTOM

The rainforest has different "layers," from the tippy-top of the tallest trees to the dark forest floor. Each layer has its own plants and animals. At the top is the emergent layer. Huge trees soar hundreds of feet into the air—they're tall because they reach for the sun. These trees are green and their leaves are plump thanks to a lot of rain. Eagles, monkeys, bats, and butterflies live in this layer. Just below is the canopy, often called the "roof" of the rainforest because it creates shade and offers shelter from the elements. A huge range of animals call the canopy their home, including snakes, toucans, and tree frogs. The next layer down is the understory. Because not much sunlight reaches this area, the trees and plants that grow here have big leaves to capture as much light as they can. Jaguars, tree frogs, and leopards dwell here. At the very bottom is the forest floor, where almost no plants grow because barely any sunlight filters all the way down. This layer's wet, hot conditions mean that things that fall down here decay very quickly. A leaf that might take a year to decompose in a regular climate can disappear here in just six weeks!

EMERGENT LAYER

CANOPY

UNDERSTORY

FOREST FLOOR

Rainforests help create the whole world's weather patterns. Water that evaporates from trees in the rainforest falls in other places as rain.

Bet You Didn't Know!

The orchid mantis, which looks just like the flower it's named for, can live only near orchids in the rainforests of Southeast Asia. It crouches there, perfectly mimicking a flower, waiting for an unwitting insect to zoom in for a taste of nectar. Then—snap!

125

Some moths make their home in sloths' fur.

A three-toed sloth is soaked after a downpour in Gamboa, Panama.

RAIN RENEGADE:
THREE-TOED SLOTH

What's brown and furry and green all over? A sloth! Even though their long hair is brown, three-toed sloths move so slowly that there is plenty of time for a layer of slimy algae and fungi to grow on their backs and arms. Algae thrives in the rainforest climate: More than 80 different types can grow on a sloth while it hangs from the trees. That living layer helps camouflage the sloth against the green foliage of the Central and South American rainforest it calls home.

The sloth's rainy home has another odd effect on its fur: It makes it grow in reverse! A sloth's hair parts in the center of its belly and grows up, toward its back. Even the hair on its face points upward! That's the opposite direction of every other mammal. Their hair is this way because sloths spend their lives upside down. When it rains, this hair pattern helps water run off their bodies.

Sloths move slower than any other mammal. But they're not being lazy: They owe their easygoing lifestyle to their limited diet of leaves and a slow metabolism. Sloths have a large, four-chambered stomach (like a cow's) that uses bacteria to digest leaves. It can take weeks for a sloth to digest a single leaf!

Sloths stay in trees most of the time because, on the forest floor, they are in great danger: On the ground, their weak hind legs provide almost no power and their long claws make walking difficult. They have to drag themselves along the rainforest floor by digging in with their front claws and dragging their bellies across the ground. This makes them an easy target for predators such as jaguars, large birds of prey, and snakes. But while in trees, sloths' algae-covered coats and slow way of moving make them nearly impossible for hungry predators to spot. No wonder some sloths will stay in the same rainforest tree for years!

FAMILY: Bradypodidae

OTHER COMMON NAMES: three-fingered sloth

GENUS: *Bradypus*

SIZE: 16–27 inches (40–69 cm)

FOOD: leaves

SOCIAL NETWORK: loners, except mothers with young

HABITAT: tree canopy

RANGE: Central and South America

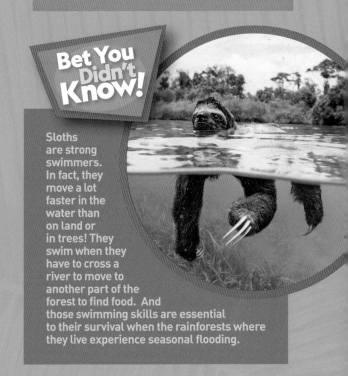

Bet You Didn't Know!

Sloths are strong swimmers. In fact, they move a lot faster in the water than on land or in trees! They swim when they have to cross a river to move to another part of the forest to find food. And those swimming skills are essential to their survival when the rainforests where they live experience seasonal flooding.

SHELTER-SEEKER:
BLUE MORPHO BUTTERFLY

Slurp, slurp, slurp. A blue morpho butterfly is dining on a piece of rotting fruit. Back when it was a caterpillar, the butterfly had jaws that it could use to chew. But now that it has shape-shifted into a butterfly, it relies on its personal straw, also called a proboscis. A blue morpho can "smell" fruit, tree sap, fungi, and other tasty delights with sensors in its antennae and legs. Imagine sticking your foot into the fridge every morning to decide what to eat for breakfast!

These brilliant blue butterflies' color makes them perfectly suited to their rainforest home. When they're flying in the sunlight high above the treetops, their wings match the blue sky. But when they fly down to the forest floor to feed, mate, or rest, they close their wings ... and disappear. Their wings are blue only on top—the undersides are brown and dotted with spots that look like eyes. This camouflage conceals them perfectly in the dark conditions at the forest floor. It's a sneaky trick that helps scare off potential predators.

Butterflies can't fly when they get cold and wet. So when it rains—which it does a lot in the rainforest!—they hide under leaves to avoid being pelted by raindrops that might be a seventh of their body weight. (That may not sound like a lot, but it's the equivalent of a 90-pound [41-kg] kid being pelted with a medium-size bowling ball!) In between frequent rainforest showers, blue morphos flutter around in a flurry of activity, winging through the jungle canopy in search of food or mates.

FAMILY: Nymphalidae

GENUS: *Morpho*

SIZE: wingspan 3–8 inches (76–200 mm)

FOOD: adults eat rotting fruit

SOCIAL NETWORK: groups

HABITAT: rainforest

RANGE: Mexico, Central and South America

Bet You Didn't Know!

Blue morphos' eyes are highly sensitive to UV light—a kind humans can't see. When filmed with special cameras that can see UV, blue morphos' wings flash with hidden patterns. Experts think the butterflies might use these invisible markings like a secret code to communicate to other butterflies without predators knowing.

After it rains, a butterfly must dry out and warm up in the sun before it can go back to flying.

129

Madagascar is home to nearly two-thirds of all chameleon species in the world!

Parson's chameleon basking in the sun

SUPER SUN-SOAKER:
PARSON'S
CHAMELEON

A hot, wet rainforest may seem too steamy and uncomfortable to a human.

But to a chameleon, life in sauna-like surroundings is just right. In fact, because they are cold-blooded, reptiles are found only in the world's temperate and tropical zones. Parson's chameleons—the largest chameleons in the world—live on the island of Madagascar, in Africa, where the rainforest gets about 150 inches (381 cm) of precipitation each year.

Like all reptiles, chameleons are cold-blooded, which means that they can't regulate their own body temperature and have to use the heat of the sun to warm their bodies. The chameleon's incredible color-changing abilities help it with temperature control: If a chameleon gets chilly, it can make its skin darker, helping it soak up more heat from the sun to warm up. If it gets too toasty, it can become paler, reflecting heat away from its body. Chameleons also use their color-change skills for camouflage and for communication with other chameleons. A male chameleon might turn deep purple to intimidate another male, or brilliant blue, orange, red, or yellow with vibrant stripes and spots to show off for a female.

Chameleons are well suited for life in the thick rainforest. They have pincers that grasp branches with what look like thumbs. Their long tongues can snatch beetles, mantises, moths, and whatever comes within reach. Their eyes can rotate nearly 180 degrees, and each one can move in a different direction at the same time, giving chameleons the ability to see almost everything around them—a handy skill when it comes to spotting the insects these animals like to snack on. When a chameleon observes a potential meal with one eye, the other eye swivels to lock on the target. Then, the chameleon shoots out its long, sticky tongue to snag the prey. Slurp!

FAMILY: Chamaeleonidae

SCIENTIFIC NAME: *Calumma parsonii*

SIZE: 19 to 24 inches (47–68 cm)

FOOD: insects

SOCIAL NETWORK: solitary

HABITAT: rainforest

RANGE: Madagascar

Bet You Didn't Know!

The veiled chameleon is a large chameleon species found in the mountain regions of Yemen and Saudi Arabia where there is very little water. Males and females differ greatly in size, with the males being much larger, although both have a decorative growth on their head that looks like a party hat but is called a casque. The casque acts like a water collector: At night, droplets of moisture roll down the casque and into the chameleon's open mouth!

WHAT DO ANIMALS DO WHEN IT RAINS?

When the skies open up, most humans take cover under umbrellas or wrap up in raincoats. But what do animals do when conditions get wet and stormy?

Some creatures seek shelter when the rains come. A leopard might hide in a cave or under a fallen log. A monkey might climb into a tree hollow to wait out the weather.

Size matters when it comes to riding out rain. Small bodies can be a big benefit: While a person won't get much shelter under a tree, little creatures such as frogs and birds can hide on the sheltered side of trees, under leaves, or inside thick foliage to stay dry and safe from the wind. Flying insects like butterflies can't fly in rain at all. They hide under tree leaves until conditions clear up, taking flight when it's hot and sunny again.

Of all animals, primates may have the most impressive tactic for staying dry. When the rain comes down, they tear off a large leaf and wear it on their heads like a hat, or hold it above themselves like an umbrella. Hmm ... Do you think the mothers of great apes make their little ones wear leaf rain boots, too?

This young orangutan in Indonesia has made an umbrella from a large leaf.

SLITHERING SNAKES

Just like chameleons and other reptiles, the warm climate of the rainforest is ideal for snakes. Without chilly winters, these cold-blooded creatures can remain active all year-round. And in the hustling, bustling rainforest, snakes have an extensive menu of prey to choose from. Some snake species are venomous, stunning and killing their prey with a quick stab of their teeth. Others wrap their bodies around their prey and crush them.

PARADISE TREE SNAKE

Snakes can't fly ... or can they? Paradise tree snakes slither up a supertall tree trunk to stalk prey—such as lizards and bats—from above. They make their way to the narrowest branch and then launch themselves into the air! Using its muscular body, the snake glides some 330 feet (100 m) to find prey, which it kills by both injecting venom into it and constricting it. Luckily, in the rainforest there are plenty of branches for landing. Incoming!

FALSE TREE CORAL SNAKE

Some rainforest snakes aren't dangerous at all ... they only pretend to be. Found in a few South American rainforests, the non-venomous false tree coral snake sports black, red, and yellow stripes designed to make it look like the truly deadly venomous coral snake. Potential predators see the snake's pattern and stay away—not knowing they've just encountered a sneaky mimic.

WHITE-LIPPED ISLAND PIT VIPER

Don't be fooled by the stunning blue color of the white-lipped island pit viper. It is beautiful—but it's deadly. Fangs inject venom when these hunters bite their prey, which can be any small creature from a lizard to a bird. These stealthy snakes are found on only a few islands in Indonesia.

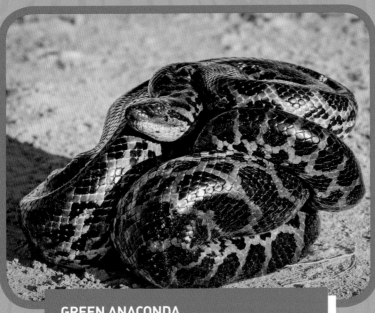

GREEN ANACONDA

Anacondas make good use of the bounty of the Amazon rainforest in South America. Green anacondas are the largest snakes by weight in the world, growing to be up to 550 pounds (250 kg)! Anacondas can take down almost any animal in their range, from wild pigs to caimans, by ambushing from hiding spots in muddy ground and shallow rivers. Anacondas sense vibrations in the ground to know when potential prey is nearby. An anaconda constricts its muscular body around its prey until its blood supply is cut off—and then it swallows the animal whole.

THE FOREST FLOOR

Everything that falls in the rainforest winds up on its dark, damp floor. Dead leaves and branches settle to the bottom, as does the poop from animals in the trees above. That may sound gross, but it's very nutritious for the plants that grow here.

The rainforest's hot, humid conditions make it an ideal environment for microbes such as bacteria and fungi. These teeny organisms munch away at dead leaves and animal waste, breaking them down into their basic components (such as carbon and nitrogen) in a process called decomposition. These chemicals then soak into the soil, where they are absorbed by plants and trees. Animals eat this foliage, and the cycle starts all over again.

135

SUPER SURVIVOR: COLLARED PECCARY

Pee-yew! What is that musky smell?!

There must be a peccary nearby. Also called musk hogs, these pig-size mammals will squeal and emit a strong scent from a gland on their rump when they are startled. Peccaries rub their bodies on trees to mark their territories with this unusual odor.

Scent helps peccaries communicate with each other in the dense rainforests throughout Central America to northern Argentina where they live. Some peccaries also make their home in the deserts of the southern United States. In their habitats, the temperature drops at night. Because peccaries are sensitive to cold, they huddle together in shelters such as caves to keep warm.

Peccaries are great at surviving in a variety of climates because they are not picky eaters: They are omnivores, meaning they will eat just about anything. Plants, nuts, fruits, insects, snakes, and small mammals are all on the menu. In the desert, peccaries dine mostly on agave plants and prickly pear cactus. These foods are high in water, helping desert peccaries keep from getting too thirsty in their hot home.

Peccaries make a lot of noise—barking, grunting, purring, woofing, and coughing—because they have good hearing but poor vision and rely on sound to communicate. When threatened, they will stand in a group, clack their teeth, and charge. By working together, they can scare off bigger predators—even coyotes.

FAMILY: Tayassuidae

OTHER COMMON NAMES : musk hog, javelina

SCIENTIFIC NAME: *Pecari tajacu*

SIZE: Up to 3.3 feet (1 m) long and weighing up to 55 pounds (25 kg)

FOOD: insects, roots, fruits, plants

SOCIAL NETWORK: family groups

HABITAT: flooded grasslands; rainforests

RANGE: North, Central, and South America

Bet You Didn't Know!

Because of their razor-sharp teeth, peccaries were nicknamed javelinas by Spanish explorers, after the Spanish word for spear.

Peccaries are mostly nocturnal in the hotter months of the summer.

A collared peccary munches on a cactus.

137

Bet You Didn't Know!

Not all parrots live in warm climates. Some species are adapted to withstand chilly weather. The kea, for example, lives in the snowy mountains of New Zealand.

WILD ABOUT WATER:
SCARLET MACAW

Bright red, yellow, and blue ... a rainbow of colors moves across the sky as a flock of scarlet macaws takes to the air. They have just woken up high in the tree tops of a rainforest in Peru. Time to find some breakfast of nuts, berries, seeds, and leaves.

Macaws are the largest parrots in the world—a scarlet macaw can be as long as 33 inches (84 cm) from beak to tail. They have strong wings that can send them speeding through the air at 35 miles an hour (56 km/h). Combine their size with their bright colors, and scarlet macaws are hard to miss. But you might be surprised to know that those bright colors actually blend in with the green leaves, red and yellow fruits, and bluish shadows of the rainforest. And it's a good thing they love water! In the wild, macaws get plenty of showers from the constant rain of their tropical habitat.

Scarlet macaws will eat the many kinds of fruit that grow in the warm, wet rainforest. There's a lot of competition for rainforest fruits, so macaws get an edge by eating fruit that isn't quite ripe yet. Unripe fruit often contains compounds that can make animals sick—but macaws have no problem. Macaws eat a lot of clay from riverbeds, and experts think that the clay may neutralize, or cancel out, the unripe fruit's nasty chemicals so the birds don't get sick.

FAMILY: Psittacidae

SCIENTIFIC NAME: *Ara macao*

SIZE: 33 inches (84 cm) beak to tail

FOOD: fruits, nuts, and seeds; plants, insects, clay

SOCIAL NETWORK: flocks except when paired for nesting

HABITAT: rainforest

RANGE: Mexico, Central and South America

Macaws are known for their noisy nature. Their loud squawks make their presence known in the rainforest. They scream to communicate to each other, claim territory, and even just for fun.

ON TOP OF THE TROPICS: SPIDER MONKEY

If you walk through the rainforest and are suddenly bombarded with branches from above, chances are there are spider monkeys nearby! Spider monkeys are known to hurl anything they can grab to defend their territory from invaders.

These primates live in the thick canopy of the rainforest, swinging from branch to branch and walking along high limbs with ease. They can travel long distances through the canopy without ever touching the ground! A spider monkey's tail is like another arm: It uses it to hang from branches and to pick fruit. When they stretch out their long arms and legs plus their tail, these primates look like spiders in the trees overhead.

Monkeys thrive in the tropics, where lots of rainfall means lush fruit trees that have plenty for them to eat. But in recent years, cold and extra-wet spells in some tropical areas have been too much for them to handle. In 2005, scientists in the Costa Rican rainforest found that an unusual number of monkeys, along with other animals such as toucans, macaws, and sloths, did not survive that year. As many animals normally hunker down and wait out the rain, excessive downpours may have made it impossible for them to forage, and they couldn't gather enough food to survive. Scientists aren't sure why this happened, but they believe extreme weather events like these may be related to climate change.

Spider monkeys love to socialize. During the day, they gather in groups of up to three dozen animals, communicating with screeches and barks while they forage in the treetops for nuts, fruits, leaves, bird eggs, and spiders. They love to play and wrestle. A baby spider monkey clings tightly to its mother's back as she moves through the rainforest. Sometimes, it wraps its little tail around mom's for extra security!

FAMILY: Atelidae

OTHER COMMON NAMES: Geoffroy's spider monkey

SCIENTIFIC NAME: *Ateles geoffroyi*

SIZE: 12–25 inches (31–63 cm), with a 25–33 inch (64–84 cm) tail

FOOD: ripe fruit, seeds, nuts, flowers

SOCIAL NETWORK: groups of 30

HABITAT: tropical rainforest

RANGE: Mexico and Central America

Bet You Didn't Know!

Spider monkeys and some other rainforest animals dine on a buffet of rainforest fruits. They digest the flesh, but not the seeds, which drop to the ground inside the monkey's poop. Many seeds can't sprout if they don't pass through the gut of a monkey or other animal first. And once they sprout, the poop helps provide nutrients for growth that the forest floor lacks because of the constant rainfall.

CHAPTER 8

LIFE IN THE DESERT ZONES

The sun rises over the desert's sand dunes like a ball of fire. As it climbs into the sky, the temperature rises—fast. Heat makes the air above the ground shimmer. The sun's rays beat down on the ground, evaporating all traces of water. There's almost nothing to eat or drink here. Yet even in this barren landscape, there is life. People have lived here for thousands of years, setting up temporary tent villages, then moving on to the next spot when they've used up the area's food and water. And all kinds of animals make the desert their home, too, from long-legged camels to a tiny beetle with a special shell.

A fennec fox in Morocco

Bactrian camels in the
Gobi desert, Mongolia

CLIMATE IN THE DESERT

Deserts are found on every continent on the planet, and they cover more than one-fifth of Earth's land. A desert is a place that receives less than 10 inches (25 cm) of rain per year. Often, deserts actually lose more moisture through evaporation than they gain through rainfall. No wonder people sometimes say "dry as a desert!"

Most deserts exist in the Earth's low latitudes—about 30 degrees north and south of the Equator. One of these, the Sahara in northern Africa, is the largest hot desert in the world. Here, temperatures can climb to 122°F (50°C) during the day. But at night, the desert becomes very cold, with temperatures in many deserts dropping to well below freezing.

Many people think of deserts as hot places. But did you know that there are cold deserts, too? Cold deserts are found on high, flat areas, called plateaus, in some of the world's temperate regions. The Gobi desert in Central Asia is one of the coldest deserts in the world. Here, temperatures can drop to -40°F (-40°C).

You might think that because there's almost no rain in the desert, there wouldn't be storms, either. But that's not true: In the desert, storms are swirling clouds of dust and sand. They happen when dry winds blowing up to 60 miles an hour (100 km/h) whip up walls of debris that can reach up to 20,000 feet (6,100 m) high. In 2006, a giant sandstorm in the Gobi scooped up 330,700 tons (300,000 t) of sand, then carried it more than 1,000 miles (1,600 km) before it dumped the sand on Beijing, China!

DRYING OUT

Some of the world's dry areas are turning into deserts in a process called desertification. As humans have settled into these regions, they have cleared the land's natural vegetation to plant their crops or by grazing their animals, as happened in this field in Bình Thuận Province, Vietnam. Without plants to hold it in place, the soil is loosened, then blown away by wind or washed away by rain—a process called erosion. Over time, the fertile land is turned into a desert. Experts think warming temperatures caused by climate change could be speeding up the process of desertification. Some say that in the future, more than a quarter of the planet's surface could become desert.

Bet You Didn't Know!

Antarctica is considered a desert because it gets very little rain or snow. In addition to being the coldest continent on Earth, Antarctica is also the driest and the windiest.

LOST IN THE DESERT

Mauro Prosperi was an expert athlete—a former Olympian in the sport of pentathlon, an event involving fencing, swimming, riding, shooting, and cross-country running. So in 1994, when he heard about an endurance race through the Sahara, he was up for the challenge.

The Marathon des Sables is a six-day, 155-mile (250-km) trek through the desert in southern Morocco, often described as the toughest race on Earth. For its participants, it's the equivalent of running five-and-a-half marathons in temperatures that can reach 122°F (50°C)! Runners have to carry their own supplies, including a week's worth of food, an emergency snakebite kit, a penknife, and a distress flare, in addition to personal items. The only thing the competitors don't have to carry in their packs is water, which is supplied at race checkpoints (though runners do carry a small amount).

Today, up to 1,300 athletes compete in the Marathon des Sables. But in 1994, when Prosperi entered, there were only 80. That meant that most of the time he was running, he was running alone. That's the solo situation he found himself in on the race's fourth day, when things went wrong.

Prosperi had passed through four checkpoints and was making his way through an area of sand dunes when the wind picked up. The swirled-up sand whipped at Prosperi, feeling like needles against his face. He was suddenly in the middle of a violent sandstorm! Prosperi turned his back to the wind and wrapped a scarf around his face so he could keep breathing. To keep from being buried where he stood, he had to move forward until he found a sheltered spot, where he crouched and waited out the storm. Eight long hours later, the wind finally quieted. It was dark, and so Prosperi slept on the dunes. It wasn't until he woke up the next morning that he realized he had a problem.

Nothing around Prosperi looked familiar. He had a map and a compass, but there were no landmarks to orient himself. When he climbed a dune and realized there were no signs of civilization anywhere around him, Prosperi began to grow worried. He only had half a bottle of water left.

Prosperi was as careful as possible. He rested during the day when temperatures were highest, walking only at night, and conserved every drop of water he could. On the second day, he heard a helicopter overhead. Prosperi shot his distress flare into the sky, but the pilot didn't see him.

Days into his ordeal, Prosperi found a shrine, where he took shelter and waited, hoping someone would spot the flag he had planted on the roof. Three days later, he heard an airplane flying close. Desperate to be spotted, he lit his backpack on fire, hoping the pilot would see the smoke. But then, another sandstorm hit, blotting out the sky. The airplane flew on. Panicked, Prosperi felt sure he was going to die. So, in a last, desperate attempt to survive, he decided he would leave his shelter and start walking.

Prosperi trekked the desert for days, killing snakes and lizards he found and eating them raw. He squeezed the juice out of desert plants called succulents. He was dangerously dehydrated, but he kept going. On the eighth day since the fateful sandstorm, he came across an oasis in the desert. As he lay there sipping water, he spotted a footprint in the sand; the sight filled him with hope that people might be close. After eight days lost in the desert, Prosperi stumbled upon a tribe of Berber nomads. They gave him goat's milk and alerted the police, who came to the rescue.

Prosperi had wandered over the border into Algeria—an astounding 181 miles (291 km) off-course. He had lost 35 pounds (16 kg). His eyes and liver were damaged, and it took him almost two years to fully recover. But he survived, and, four years later, he was back in Morocco at the starting line of the Marathon des Sables, ready to take on the desert that had once almost killed him.

OPPOSITE: Prosperi only hours before the sandstorm in which he would become lost; Prosperi after his rescue (inset)

TOP: Map of the 1994 race

ABOVE: Where Prosperi took shelter

PEOPLE IN THE DESERT

With soaring temperatures and lack of water, deserts are undoubtedly harsh places. Some deserts are among the last areas of total wilderness left on Earth—uncultivated and uninhabited. Many deserts are barren and desolate, but that doesn't mean they're too harsh for humans. In fact, more than one billion people call deserts home.

The desert is a place of extremes. Many desert people have to survive scorching hot days that turn into frigid nights. Dust storms thousands of feet high can cover everything in a wall of whipping dirt. One legend says that around 530 B.C., the king of the Persian Empire Cambyses II sent an army of 50,000 men across the desert in western Egypt, where they were swallowed by an enormous sandstorm and never seen again. Archaeologists have been searching the Sahara for the "Lost Army of Cambyses" ever since.

And when the rains do come, flash floods can wipe out entire areas. In most places, rainwater drains into rivers, lakes, or oceans. But many deserts don't have these bodies of water to collect overflow, so rainwater can cover the landscape with little warning. In 2009, the city of Jeddah in Saudi Arabia was struck with a flash flood that washed away roads and buildings and caused the deaths of more than 100 people.

AMAZING ADAPTATIONS

People have been living in the desert for thousands of years. In that time, they've developed all kinds of tools and technologies to help them survive. But their bodies have changed, too, adapting to desert conditions. Humans' bodies in general are very good at keeping cool. Unlike many animals, we sweat: The evaporation of sweat from the surface of the skin lowers body temperature. Indigenous people who live in the desert, such as the bushmen of South Africa (below), are often thin, which helps their bodies radiate the maximum amount of heat. And because having dark skin helps protect from the sun's radiation but also absorbs a lot of heat, indigenous desert people often have skin that is moderately dark in color.

Bet You Didn't Know!

In the world's driest deserts, it almost never rains. Some weather stations in South America's Atacama Desert, for example, have never recorded a drop of rain! The Atacama receives less than half an inch (1 cm) of precipitation each year in the form of fog, not rain. There, people use giant mesh nets called fog catchers, such as this one shown (left) in Lima, Peru, to collect the fog from the air for drinking and to water crops.

A haboob advances over
Khartoum, Sudan.

AT HOME IN THE DESERT ZONES

What is EVERYDAY LIFE like for people in the desert?

HERDING CAMELS

Animals such as camels are naturally adapted to surviving in the hot desert climate. Nomadic desert people herd these animals from place to place as they travel the desert. Many desert people drink camel milk, an important source of water and nutrients in a place where both are scarce.

HUNTING WITH EAGLES

For hundreds of years, the nomadic Mongolian people of the Gobi desert have hunted with the help of golden eagles. Eagle hunters, such as these in western Mongolia, spend months training the birds of prey to catch animals such as rabbits, then bring them back to the hunter for a food reward.

WEARING PROTECTIVE CLOTHING

Desert people traditionally wear long, loose clothing that allows air to circulate while protecting them from the sun. Head coverings such as turbans and veils (such as the one worn by this Bedouin woman) help shield them, too, and also keep debris out of their eyes, nose, and ears when sandstorms strike.

MODERN MARVEL

Humans don't always change their lifestyles to suit the place they live. Sometimes, they use technology to change the place they live instead! Las Vegas, Nevada, is lush and green even though it's in the middle of the Mojave Desert. That's because 90 percent of the city's drinking water is piped in from the Lake Mead reservoir about 25 miles (40 km) away, which is fed by the Colorado River. But environmentalists warn that there isn't enough water to replenish what Las Vegas is using, such as what it takes to keep this desert golf course green.

KEEPING COOL AT HOME

Desert-dwelling people, including the Bedouins, traditionally make their homes in tents, like this one in Jordan's Wadi Rum desert. Tents allow air to flow inside, keeping them cool during the day. And animal hair can be used to insulate the tents, keeping them warm when temperatures drop at night.

ON THE MOVE

Many indigenous people of the desert, such as the Bedouins, traditionally live a nomadic lifestyle. From North Africa to the Middle East, they are always on the move, traveling to one place and then moving on to another when all the food and water have been used up.

WHERE DID SUNSCREEN COME FROM?

You probably don't think twice about smoothing on a layer of sunscreen before you head out to the beach or pool during the summertime. But have you ever wondered how people protected themselves from the sun's rays before modern sunscreen was invented?

Paintings show that ancient Greeks used veils and hats with big brims to shade themselves. The ancient Greeks also used olive oil for sun protection, and some American Indian tribes used a kind of pine needle called *Tsuga canadensis,* which was helpful in relieving sunburns. Papyrus scrolls and tomb walls show that ancient Egyptians rubbed plant extracts onto their bodies in an attempt to stave off sunburn. Interestingly, modern science shows that some of their ingredients actually worked—rice bran, for example, absorbs UV light, and jasmine can help repair damaged DNA.

Developed in the late 1800s, the first bathing suits offered nearly full body protection by covering the skin from neck to ankle. Over time, as bathing suits got smaller, sunburns became more common. But it wasn't until World War II that the search for sunscreen took off in earnest. American soldiers stationed in the Philippines needed a way to protect their skin while they worked on aircraft carrier decks under the blazing sun. So, the government began experimenting with sun-blocking substances.

One of the first substances, invented by an airman and pharmacist named Benjamin Green, was red petrolatum, a heavy, red jelly left behind after the process of making gasoline from crude oil. It was unpleasant to wear, but it worked. After the war, Green tweaked the ingredients until he had a creamy lotion people could spread on their skin. That invention eventually became Coppertone sunscreen—and people have been slathering it on ever since.

Bet You Didn't Know!

Many sunscreens contain chemicals that are harmful to marine life. Oxybenzone, for example, which is widely used in sunscreen because it absorbs UV rays, can cause coral bleaching and deformities in young corals. Some companies are now taking note, however, and making sunscreens that are safer for coral reefs by using alternative UV blocking ingredients, such as non-nano titanium dioxide.

ANIMALS OF THE DESERT

If you have ever spent any time in a desert, you were probably grateful every chance you got to take refuge from the heat inside an air-conditioned building.

But most desert creatures can't escape their climate; instead, they have had to become experts in surviving their hot home.

Animals adapted to desert life have a special name: xerocoles. All kinds of animals, from insects to reptiles to birds to mammals, can be xerocoles. They are creatures built to survive in their extreme environment.

Xerocoles have bodies that have evolved over millions of years to help them beat the heat. Jackrabbits, for example, have long ears packed with blood vessels that release lots of heat, cooling the animals down. Kangaroo rats burrow underground to escape high temperatures. Tortoises have thick shells that protect their bodies from the sun's rays.

They've also developed amazing adaptations to deal with the desert's water shortage. Some, like dorcas gazelles, found in North Africa and the Middle East, get all the water they need to survive from the plants they eat. The North American kangaroo rat takes conserving water to the extreme: As it exhales, it filters the water vapor in its breath out through special organs in its nose, then recycles that water into its body.

DESERT PLANTS

Desert plants also have ingenious techniques for survival. Many plants on Earth have large leaves to help them capture sunlight, which they use to make energy in a process called photosynthesis. But these plants release lots of water vapor through their leaves—not a good idea when water is scarce. So almost all desert plants have tiny, waxy leaves instead. And some don't have leaves at all: Cactuses soak up water and store it in their trunks. Saguaro cactuses, which live in the Sonoran Desert of Arizona (above) and northern Mexico, have pleated surfaces that expand like accordions when there is a rainstorm. A large saguaro is like a living water tower that can hold 200 gallons (750 l) of water!

Bet You Didn't Know!

The desert might seem empty of life during the day. But try visiting at night! Most xerocoles, including foxes, rodents (such as this banner-tailed kangaroo rat), and coyotes, are nocturnal, meaning that they sleep during the day when temperatures are hottest and are awake at night when the desert cools down.

This black-tailed jackrabbit is actually not a rabbit at all: It's a desert hare that can be found in the western United States and Mexico. Hares are larger and have longer ears than rabbits.

155

Fennec foxes have the largest ears relative to their body size of any member of the canid family.

HEAT-RELEASING EARS:
FENNEC FOX

The first thing you notice when you see a fennec fox is its oversize ears. They look like they were borrowed from a much bigger animal! But this desert fox's ears aren't just for looks: They actually help the fox survive in its hot home. Besides helping the fox listen for prey underground, the ears also help keep the fox cool by releasing excess body heat.

Fennec foxes live throughout the deserts of the Sahara and North Africa. They live a lifestyle adapted to the extreme heat of their environment: They have long, thick hair that shields them from the sun during the day and keeps them warm when the temperature drops at night. Even the fox's feet are furry, which helps protect them from the hot ground. They also act like snowshoes, helping the fox move gracefully across shifting sands.

Like many desert creatures, fennec foxes escape the heat by spending the daytime in burrows under the sand. At up to three feet (1 m) deep, the burrows stay cool while the sun scorches the ground above. Fennec foxes live in communities of around 10 individuals and often build their burrows so that they connect to each other's via tunnels.

After snoozing the day away, fennec foxes come out at dusk to hunt in the cool of the night. They are masters of stealth and lie in wait to ambush their favorite meals, including insects, rodents, and lizards. Like many desert-dwelling creatures, fennec foxes need very little water and get most of what they need from plants. Now that's a smart survival strategy!

FAMILY: Canidae

SCIENTIFIC NAME: *Vulpes zerda*

SIZE: up to 16 inches (40 cm)

FOOD: eggs, insects, rodents, reptiles

SOCIAL NETWORK: small groups

HABITAT: desert

RANGE: North Africa and Sinai Peninsula

OPPOSITE: Fennec fox cub

ABOVE: Fennec fox pups playing outside their den in Tunisia, Africa

LEFT: Fennec fox emerging from its burrow in Libya

ADAPTED TO EXTREMES:
BACTRIAN CAMEL

Many people think a camel's humps store water. That would make sense for an animal that can survive for weeks without drinking. But it's not true! This desert-dweller's humps actually store fat. That allows Bactrian camels to last several months without food. As the camel's body uses up the fat in its hump, the hump becomes droopy and floppy.

Camels rarely sweat, which helps them conserve fluids so they can go for long periods of time without drinking. When camels do get a chance to drink, they can slurp down an incredible amount of water. A very thirsty camel can drink 30 gallons (114 l) of water in only 13 minutes. That's nearly enough to fill a bathtub!

Bactrian camels live in the Gobi desert of China and the steppes of Mongolia. Here, the climate is truly extreme: Summers can be blazing hot, with temperatures rising above 100°F (38°C), while winters can be very cold, dropping to -20°F (-29°C). Bactrian camels have a whole host of adaptations that help them survive these climate shifts. They have a shaggy brown coat that changes with the season. During winter, it thickens to help the camels keep warm. Then, in the summer, the camels shed large clumps of fur to help them stay cool.

Bactrian camels even have special adaptations that help them survive when sandstorms rage across their desert home. They have double rows of extra-long eyelashes (right) and ears lined with hair to shield them. Camels can even pinch their nostrils shut to keep out blowing sand!

FAMILY: Camelidae

SCIENTIFIC NAME: *Camelus ferus*

SIZE: more than 7 feet (2.1 m) tall at the hump

FOOD: desert plants

SOCIAL NETWORK: herds

HABITAT: Gobi desert

RANGE: Mongolia and China

Bet You Didn't Know!

Wild Bactrian camels are the only truly wild camel species left on Earth. Having been heavily hunted for years in their desert habitat, they are also now critically endangered. The vast majority of the world's camels are domesticated dromedary camels, used as livestock or as working animals.

Bactrian camels have two humps. Dromedaries, also called Arabian camels, have only one.

Bactrian camel in the Mongolian desert

Similar to the fogstand beetle, the Australian thorny devil lizard collects dew in the grooves on its skin.

A desert darkling beetle collects fog water droplets in the tiny ridges of its hardened wings in Swakopmund, Dorob National Park, Namibia.

EXPERT WATER HARVESTER:
NAMIB DESERT BEETLE

It almost never rains in the Namib desert of Namibia in Africa. And the only water around isn't easy for most animals to access: Here, wind blows moist air from the Atlantic Ocean to form a fog that floats above the ground. The water is trapped in this low cloud—out of reach.

Namib desert animals have adapted in different ways. Some, such as the hairy thick-tailed scorpion and the Namaqua chameleon, get the moisture they need from eating other animals. Shovel-snouted lizards drink fog off their bodies or stones—and store the water in a second bladder! But Namib desert beetles may have the most industrious approach of all. These creepy-crawlies have a survival superpower: harvesting water from the fog! The beetle stands up on its long hind legs, sticking its back—which is covered with a complex series of bumps and troughs—into the air, its head facing upwind and its stiff, bumpy outer wings spread out against the damp breeze. Water droplets collect on the beetle's back, accumulating until they're big enough to roll down the troughs right to its mouth.

Ever since this beetle's remarkable water-harvesting ability was discovered, scientists have been scrambling to copy it and create materials that can pull water out of thin air. One scientist combined a beetle's bump pattern with tiny ramps inspired by a cactus's spines (which are also excellent at harvesting water from the air), and a slippery coating inspired by carnivorous plants to create a material that can collect 10 times more water than other surfaces. And experts in Chile installed large mesh panels coated in the material on hillsides, hoping that someday they'll help provide water for drinking and watering crops.

FAMILY: Tenebrionidae

OTHER COMMON NAMES: fogstand beetle

SCIENTIFIC NAME:
Stenocara gracilipes

SIZE: up to 2 inches (5 cm)

FOOD: decomposing matter, plants, fungi

HABITAT: desert regions

RANGE: Namib Desert

NAMIB DESERT

AMAZING ADAPTATIONS

Many desert animals have evolved incredible ways to beat the heat. Here are some of the animal kingdom's smartest survival strategies.

SKIN STRAW

Thorny devils, lizards that live in Australia, have mouths evolved for eating ants—and ants only. The devil can't even sip or lick up water! So instead, the lizard uses a series of tiny folds on its skin that act like tubes carrying water all the way to its mouth. Thorny devils cover themselves with sand and allow their skin to suck out any moisture from rain or dew.

FEATHER SPONGE

When sandgrouse chicks get thirsty in their nests in the deserts of Asia and North Africa, their dads know what to do. The male sandgrouse flies to a nearby stream for a dip. He uses special feathers on his belly to soak up nearly three tablespoons (30 ml) of liquid, then flies back to his chicks, which then use their bills like tiny squeegees to squeeze the water into their waiting beaks.

SALTY TEARS

Most animals get rid of excess salt in their bodies through urine. But that means losing water as well—and in the desert, you don't want to waste precious fluid. So the greater roadrunner of North America has a different strategy: The bird "cries" out extra salt from a gland near its eye.

RAIN COAT

When the rainy season ends on the savanna, the African bullfrog employs a nifty trick. It burrows down into the soil and sheds several layers of skin, forming a cocoon that covers its entire body, leaving only its nostrils exposed to breathe. There, the frog hibernates for up to 10 months, waiting out the dry season. When the rains return, the frog wakes up, climbs out of its odd outfit and hops away.

TAIL PARASOL

When the sun beats down on the deserts of southern Africa, the cape ground squirrel doesn't head for shade—it carries its own shade with it! This burrowing rodent holds its bushy tail over its body, using it like a parasol.

Emperor penguins
in Antarctica

CHAPTER 9

LIFE AT THE POLES

At the planet's very top and very bottom, the weather gets extreme. Ice stretches as far as the eye can see. Snow blankets everything. Sometimes screaming winds lift the snow high into the sky, whiting out the landscape for days at a time. It's incredibly cold here—much, much colder than the inside of your freezer. Yet, even in our world's most frigid corners, life endures. The ocean teems with fish and other marine life. Penguins and polar bears make a home on the frozen earth. And people live here, too—about four million of them call the wintery wonderland of the Arctic their home.

Two polar bear cubs frolic in the snow in Manitoba, Canada.

CLIMATE AT THE POLES

Antarctica, home of the South Pole, is a continent, covered by the vast Antarctic Ice Sheet—the largest single piece of ice on Earth.

As the seasons here change from summer to winter, the ice surface grows, increasing in size from 1.2 million square miles (3 million sq km) to 7.3 million square miles (19 million sq km). That's bigger than all of South America! The Antarctic Ice Sheet holds about 90 percent of all the freshwater on Earth. This stretch of ice is broken up by huge mountains, with some rising more than 14,764 feet (4,500 m) into the frigid air.

Antarctica is the coldest and windiest place on Earth. The lowest temperature recorded here is -128.6°F (-89.2°C). The cooling effect of Antarctica's ice produces very cold, dense air that blows downhill from areas of high elevation. These katabatic winds interact with a belt of low pressure that surrounds Antarctica, increasing in strength to create winds that blast faster than 62 miles an hour (100 km/h), with gusts of 124 miles an hour (200 km/h) or higher! During blizzards, blowing snow can obscure everything for days at a time—a condition called whiteout.

The Arctic, where the North Pole is located, includes the Arctic Ocean, neighboring seas, Finland, Greenland, Iceland, Norway, Russia, Sweden, Northern Canada, and parts of the U.S. state of Alaska. Much of the Arctic is covered by snow and ice. Some of that ice stays frozen all year-round, but, like in the Antarctic, much of it melts every summer and re-forms when temperatures drop again in the winter.

The Arctic isn't quite as cold as the Antarctic. While Antarctica is land surrounded by oceans, the Arctic is an ocean almost completely surrounded by land. All that water is very cold, but it's still much, much warmer than the frigid air—so its heat keeps the Arctic warmer. But that doesn't mean it's a good place to take a beach vacation: During the warmest part of summer, the temperature hits only about 32°F (0°C). Brrr!

MELTING ICE

Sea ice plays an important role in Earth's climate. Its bright white surface means that a huge amount of sunlight that strikes the ice—about 80 percent—is reflected back into space. This process, known as the albedo effect, bounces heat away from the planet, cooling it down. But as Earth's temperature has increased due to global warming, the amount of sea ice has shrunk. As sea ice disappears, there is less of it to reflect heat away from the planet, and the more the planet heats up. The amount of sea ice has reached record lows in the past few years. And, in 2018, parts of the Arctic were more than 50°F (27.8°C) warmer than normal.

Bet You Didn't Know!

Because of Earth's tilt, the North Pole stays in full sunlight all day in the summer. The sun never sets! This gives the Arctic its nickname, "the Land of the Midnight Sun." During the same time of year at the South Pole, the sun never rises.

RACE TO THE SOUTH POLE

LEFT: Captain Robert Falcon Scott (center, standing) at the South Pole with his crew. Among the flags they found was the Norwegian flag planted by Roald Amundsen a month earlier.

BELOW: Polar explorer Roald Amundsen

By the early 20th century, humans had yet to explore one of the planet's most vast and distant wildernesses: the South Pole. In 1911, two explorers faced off to become the first to reach the planet's frozen tip.

One of the competitors was British explorer Robert Falcon Scott, who had attempted to reach the South Pole once before, in 1902. But the below-freezing conditions combined with health problems on his team forced him to turn back. Scott vowed to return, and, in 1910, he set off for Antarctica. But

when he stopped in Australia along the way to take on his final supplies, he got a surprise—a telegram informing him that he had competition.

The opposition was veteran Norwegian explorer Roald Amundsen. Amundsen had spent most of his life testing his survival skills in the world's most extreme places: He was the first man in history to sail the treacherous Northwest Passage between the Atlantic and Pacific Oceans, in a voyage that lasted from

Scott's expedition members in Antarctica working with a scientific balloon

1903 to 1906. While in the Arctic, he had learned how to survive in polar conditions from the indigenous Inuit people. In fact, Amundsen's original goal was to be the first to the North Pole, but when American explorers Frederick Cook and then Robert Peary claimed to have beaten him to the punch, Amundsen changed his plans and secretly steered his ship south.

Both Scott and Amundsen spent the early part of 1911 setting up stores of food and supplies along their intended (and different) routes, for their teams to use when they made the push for the pole. Then they hunkered down for the frigid winter, waiting for the weather to ease up enough to make the journey possible. On October 20, 1911, Amundsen and his team set off. Just a few days later, on November 1, Scott started the journey.

Scott and Amundsen relied on very different strategies in their attempts. Scott used a combination of sled dogs, ponies, and a few motorized tractors. But the machines broke down, and the cold proved too harsh for the ponies. Scott and his 16 men thus had to rely on putting most of their supplies on sleds and hauling them by foot through approximately 1,000 miles (1,600 km) of snow and ice. Scott planned to split his men among three teams, and have two turn back, leaving just one group of five to make the final push to the pole. Amundsen's method was simpler:

He used only five men, who traversed the snow on skis while sled dogs pulled their supplies.

Thanks to his light-and-fast strategy, Amundsen's team was able to travel more than 20 miles (32 km) per day. They used a dangerous, untested route that took them over crevasses, mountains, and glaciers, but it was a straighter path to the pole that required less distance to travel. The gamble paid off: On December 14, 1911, Amundsen planted the Norwegian flag at the South Pole.

Scott's group was much slower. Besides his longer route, he was also slowed by scientific samples that he stopped to collect. When he and his home-stretch team finally arrived at the pole more than a month later, on January 17, 1912, they were devastated to find the remains of Amundsen's camp. But their bad luck was just beginning. As they slogged slowly back through the frigid conditions, they became weak with exhaustion, frostbite, and malnutrition. First one man, then another, succumbed to the deathly cold. A few days later, Scott and the two remaining men were caught in a blizzard only 11 miles (18 km) from one of their supply caches. A few days after that, they perished in the snow.

Since then, the doomed race has become an infamous tale of the punishing conditions of one of Earth's most extreme places. Today, its two pioneering explorers are honored in the name of the South Pole's permanent research facility: the Amundsen-Scott South Pole Station (below).

PEOPLE IN THE ARCTIC

Many explorers have lost their lives trying to battle the extreme conditions at the poles. But that hasn't stopped others from making this ice-cold environment their home. Indigenous people such as the Inuit people of Canada and Greenland and the Yu'pik, Iñupiat, and Athabascan people of Alaska, U.S.A., for example, have lived in the Arctic region for thousands of years.

Traditionally, the indigenous people of the Arctic have relied on the land to survive—hunting, fishing, herding, and gathering wild plants for food. To combat the cold, they have come up with all kinds of ingenious strategies, from the clothing they wear to the houses they live in.

Many travelers to the Arctic haven't had the same success. The first visitors to this region arrived only about a thousand years ago. They were the Vikings, and they came from Scandinavia during a time of unusually warm weather on planet Earth. They settled along the south coast of Greenland, raising cattle, sheep, and goats they had brought with them, and they hunted for seal and caribou. But, after about five centuries, the weather began to cool. The land the Vikings depended on for farming and grazing their animals gradually disappeared under advancing snow and ice. By around the late 1400s, the Viking settlements in Greenland were no more.

Today, many people in the Arctic live in the same kind of modern towns and cities as their neighbors farther south. But others live in small villages very much like their ancestors did. No matter their lifestyle, people in the Arctic today are facing major changes in weather patterns as climate change causes ice and snow to melt, putting people on the coasts in danger of big storms and threatening the plants and animals that share their home.

AMAZING ADAPTATIONS

Just like indigenous people in the tropics and the desert, those in the Arctic have bodies that have become specially adapted to their environment over many generations. Arctic people are short in stature, with short arms and legs and a thicker-than-average layer of body fat. These characteristics help their bodies hold in heat—even at their fingers and toes, the body parts that are most in danger of frostbite.

Arctic people's bodies are also adapted to a very different diet from what most humans eat. A traditional Arctic meal might consist of fatty meat like seal or whale and not many fruits and vegetables, which don't often grow there. For most people on Earth, this kind of high-fat diet could cause health problems such as heart disease and diabetes. But these diseases are rare among Inuit people. In 2015, researchers discovered that Inuit people seem to have genetic differences from their neighbors to the south that allow them to digest more fat while staying healthy.

OPPOSITE: A Yu'pik man hangs salmon on a drying rack in western Alaska.

ABOVE: A Iñupiat girl cradles puppies in western Alaska.

171

AT HOME IN THE NORTH

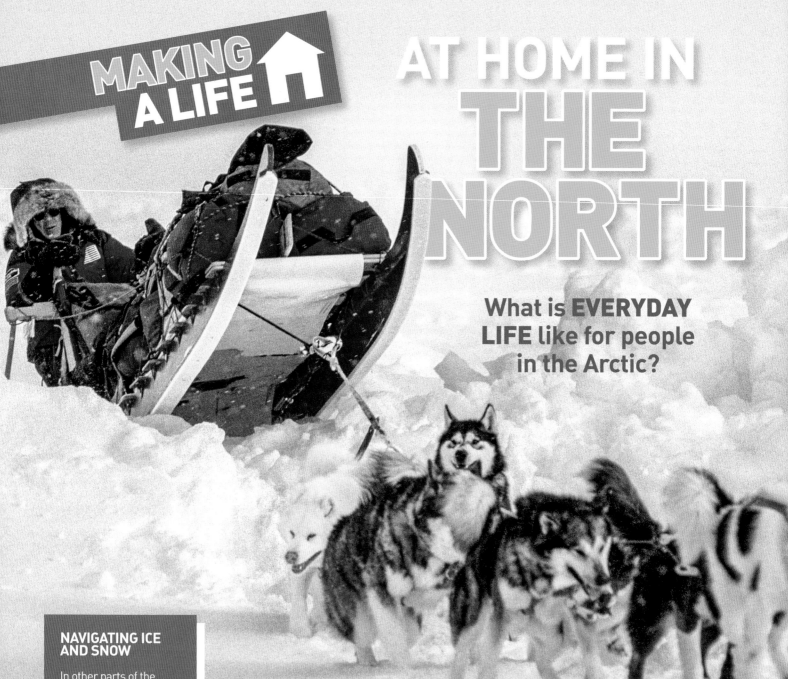

What is **EVERYDAY LIFE** like for people in the Arctic?

NAVIGATING ICE AND SNOW

In other parts of the world, people might use cars or camels to get around. But those modes of transportation aren't very effective for traveling over freezing, slippery ice. Instead, Arctic people have traditionally used snowshoes to traverse the snow without sinking in, dogsleds (such as the one above) to pull them long distances on land, and kayaks to cross water.

HUNTING FOR FOOD

Because few plants can be cultivated in the Arctic, the Inuit people have traditionally relied on animals for food. They hunt sea mammals including whales, seals, and walruses and land mammals such as caribou. They also consume fish, as well as birds and their eggs.

KEEPING WARM AT HOME

It might sound strange, but snow can keep you warm! It's a good insulator, or material that prevents heat from escaping. That's why many Arctic animals burrow under the snow to survive. Arctic people do the same thing: Igloos, dome-shaped dwellings constructed of blocks of snow, were once the traditional winter homes of some Inuit people. Warmed only by body heat, the air inside an igloo can be as high as 61°F (16°C).

INSULATING ON THE GO

Traditional Inuit clothing was designed especially to keep out the cold. Garments made of the skin of foxes, wolves, caribou, or sometimes polar bears, hold in the heat. Pants and a knee-length, parka-like coat called an anorak might be topped off with a wolf or wolverine fur hood to protect the wearer's face from snow and ice. Mittens and boots might be made of waterproof sealskin.

FISHING FOR FOOD

The Inuit people have traditionally fished using spears, harpoons, their hands, and nets strung across rivers or streams. Today, some also fish by rod and reel. In the winter, when sea ice covers the water, Inuit people cut holes in the surface and fish using lures or spears. Ancient weirs—crescent-shaped stone walls built in rivers that trap fish—can still be seen all over the Arctic.

WHY DOESN'T ANYONE LIVE IN ANTARCTICA?

The population of Antarctica is zero. Zip. None. Though the region has visitors, there are no permanent residents of this cold and windy place. But people live in other chilly parts of the world, like Alaska and Greenland. So why is Antarctica uninhabited?

About 300 million years ago, much of Earth's land was combined into one giant supercontinent called Pangaea. About 200 million years ago, Pangaea started to break apart, and current-day Antarctica began to split away from what are now Australia and South America. For the past 35 million years—long before humans appeared on the scene—there haven't been any land bridges connecting Antarctica to other continents. Isolated, surrounded by stormy seas, and with brutal weather, Antarctica was so hard to get to that ancient people never discovered it. It wasn't until 1820 that humans developed the technology to sail far enough south to even spot it for the first time.

That doesn't mean that there are no people in Antarctica. Many tourists travel to the planet's southernmost reaches to visit this desolate and wild place. But the only humans who actually stay on the continent for extended stretches of time are scientists.

Antarctica has 40 research stations, with an average of 1,000 people working in them year-round. They brave blasting winds and cold that can dip below -100°F (-73°C), all in the name of science. They observe Antarctica's organisms to learn how they are able to thrive in the deep cold, they study how the continent's climate is changing, and they observe space. (Antarctica's dry, clear air means telescopes can see very far from there.)

Working in such an extreme place has risks. Shipments of supplies only come in about every six to eight months. From February to October, the harsh weather makes flights too dangerous to attempt, so no one can leave the continent at all. Internet is spotty, and so scientists can contact home only a few times a week. And most of the research bases are hundreds of miles apart. But the scientists find ways to entertain themselves: watching movies, skiing, and even a film festival, where research bases compete to make the best amateur movies.

OPPOSITE: Tourists on the National Geographic *Endeavour* watch as the ship passes an iceberg in the Weddell Sea.

LEFT: A glaciologist takes ice cores from a snow mine below the South Pole.

The name Arctic comes from the Greek word *arktos*—meaning "land of the big bear"— after the Great Bear constellation that circles the northern sky.

Orcas are mammals that must find open pockets in icy water so they can come up for air.

ANIMALS AT THE POLES

When the temperature drops in your house, you might pull on a sweater or turn up the thermostat. Of course, the animals of the poles don't have these options. Yet all kinds of creatures, from furred to feathered, are right at home in these seemingly inhospitable regions. The Arctic Ocean is flowing with currents that move its cold water swiftly from one place to another. Those currents transport nutrients and tiny organisms, such as microscopic plants called phytoplankton. Many animals, from shrimp to fish to sea lions, thrive in this rich water. On land, the Arctic has many kinds of landscapes, including mountains, ice sheets, islands, and tundra. Here, owls soar, polar bears prowl, and caribou graze.

In Antarctica, where temperatures are truly frigid, there is little life on land. Almost no plants grow here, so there isn't much food for animals. But the ocean waters around Antarctica are a different story. Here, warm water rises from the deep sea in a process called upwelling, helping plankton and algae to flourish. Those tiny creatures feed a whole food web of marine creatures, including leopard seals, penguins, and many species of whales.

In both polar regions, animals use a range of strategies to keep warm and find food. Some of their adaptations are biological, such as the thick layers of fur and fat that help polar bears hold in their body heat. Other adaptations are behavioral. Emperor penguins, for example, have been recorded diving as deep as 1,854 feet (565 m) to seek out the abundant fish that live in their region. That's deeper than the Empire State Building is tall!

PENGUINS VS. POLAR BEARS

It might seem like polar bears and penguins frolic in the snow side by side. But thousands of miles of land and sea separate these two species—and many others that live at the poles. The Arctic region is home to polar bears, along with arctic foxes, many seals and whales, and birds such as puffins. Antarctica, on the other hand, has few native animals that live on land full time. Emperor penguins (below) and other ocean-dwelling creatures live here, along with species of whales and seals.

EXTREME COLD EXPERT: POLAR BEAR

Polar bears are masters of keeping warm in their frigid Arctic home. In fact, they're so good at staying toasty that they can easily overheat! To avoid getting too warm, polar bears tend to walk slowly unless they're hunting.

How are they built to withstand these punishingly frigid conditions? A double layer of fat up to four inches (10 cm) thick is key to their survival. Fat insulates the body, helping to keep out the -40°F (-40°C) Arctic freeze and maintain a polar bear's core temperature of 98.6°F (37°C).

On top of a polar bear's skin is a two-inch (5-cm)-thick layer of dense, short underfur. Over that, polar bears have tubelike guard hairs that can grow up to six inches (15 cm) long. Some males have foot-long (30-cm) guard hairs on their legs! These hairs trap air and help keep in heat.

Besides their layers of fat and fur, polar bears have platter-size feet that distribute their weight on the ice and increase their grip. Polar bears also have an oily coat that repels water, helping keep them warm even during a dip in the frigid Arctic waters—kind of like a built-in wet suit!

Polar bears don't hibernate like black bears. But when it's time for females to give birth, they build a nursery den, where they stay for about five months with their cubs. In many areas, polar bears dig into snow drifts on the sea ice to build their dens. But as climate change thins and shrinks sea ice, experts say more polar bear mothers have to dig dens on land instead. That means that she might not be able to get back out to sea to hunt seals when she and her tiny cubs emerge in the spring. Polar bears also hunt from sea ice, and as it thins, some bears are having to travel longer and longer distances to hunt.

FAMILY: Ursidae

SCIENTIFIC NAME: *Ursus maritimus*

SIZE: up to 8 feet (2.4 m) tall on hind legs, 900 to 1,600 pounds (408–726 kg)

FOOD: seals (ringed, ribbon, bearded), walrus, beluga whale

SOCIAL NETWORK: generally loners, except a mother and cubs

HABITAT: sea ice and land when ice melts

RANGE: Arctic

Bet You Didn't Know!

Polar bears spend most of their time at sea, even if it is frozen. They are good swimmers and have been tracked paddling across hundreds of miles of water. Scientists consider them marine mammals, along with seals, whales, dolphins, and walruses.

Unlike many other deer species, both male and female caribou can grow antlers—though not all females do.

FEET FOR ALL SEASONS:
CARIBOU

If you've ever tried to walk on snow, you know that it's sometimes hard to keep your footing on the shifting, slick surface. In the icy Arctic, getting around is also treacherous in the spring, when the snow melts and the ground becomes soft and muddy. But neither of these tricky surfaces is a problem for the caribou and its specially adapted hooves.

Also called reindeer, caribou live in the northern regions of North America, Europe, Asia, and Greenland. They have large hooves that change with—and adapt to—the seasons. In the summer, the tissues of the caribou's feet enlarge and become spongelike, giving the deer more traction on the soft, wet tundra. In the winter, this footpad shrinks, exposing their sharp-rimmed hooves—ideal for cutting into snow and ice to get a secure foothold.

It's not just the caribou's feet that vary between seasons—the animal's eyes change, too! To cope with the almost-total darkness of the Arctic winter, the backs of a caribou's eyes shift from a yellow shade to a very deep blue. This makes their eyesight more sensitive and enables caribou to see beyond the spectrum of visible light and into the ultraviolet (UV) spectrum. That super sight helps the caribou find food during the time of year when the ground—and the lichens (plants) they eat—are concealed by snow. In UV light, the food stands out. The reindeer then use their sharp hooves to dig out their meal.

And while these real-life reindeer don't have red noses, their sniffers are still pretty special. They have curled structures inside their noses that are packed with blood vessels. All these blood vessels warm up the cold air before it reaches their lungs. That helps the reindeer keep their body temperature warm and toasty—no matter how chilly it is in their frozen home.

FAMILY: Cervidae

OTHER COMMON NAMES: reindeer

SCIENTIFIC NAME: *Rangifer tarandus*

SIZE: up to 91 inches (231 cm) long, up to 700 pounds (318 kg)

FOOD: leaves, mushrooms, cotton grass, lichens

SOCIAL NETWORK: large herds in the thousands

HABITAT: Arctic tundra and subarctic forests

RANGE: just below the Arctic circle

POLAR PLUNGE

Many of the Arctic and Antarctic regions' animals make their home not on land but beneath the chilly waters of the sea.

WALRUS

These giants of the north can weigh up to 1.5 tons (1.4 t)—as much as a small car! Walruses are known for their whiskers and long tusks, and each of these features serves an important purpose: Their whiskers help them sense the vibrations of clams and mussels and other prey that dwell in the dark, deep ocean. They use their tusks to haul their huge bodies onto land and to break breathing holes in the ice.

NOTOTHENIOID FISH

The freezing cold waters that surround Antarctica are so frigid that a human would last only about 15 minutes in the 28°F (-2°C) seas. But it's no big deal for a group of fish called notothenioids, which has a secret weapon for combating the climate: natural antifreeze. Special molecules in their blood prevent ice crystals from growing, keeping the fish's blood from turning to ice, even at below-freezing temperatures.

ORCA

Orcas, also known as killer whales, are smart and social animals that often work together to hunt. In the Arctic Ocean, they've been observed using teamwork to create huge waves to knock seals off of floating ice floes and into the water for easy eating.

NARWAL

Though narwhals are sometimes called "unicorns of the sea," this animal's spiraling, swordlike tusk, which can grow nearly nine feet (3 m) long, is actually a tooth that grows right through the animal's upper lip. These relatives of the dolphin live in frozen Arctic waters, relying on breaks in the sea ice, called leads, to allow them to come up for air.

BOWHEAD WHALE

Many species of whales visit the Arctic only in the summer, migrating to warmer waters during the winter. But not the bowhead whale. This big swimmer braves the Arctic's chill with a layer of blubber that is up to two feet (0.6 m) thick.

FEATHER DEFENSE:
SNOWY OWL

The snowy owl swoops, flying straight for a lemming on the ground. The owl's wings—stretching up to five feet (1.5 m) across—make no noise as it flies. That silent swooping—and the creature's snowy white plumage—give this Arctic animal its nickname: ghost owl.

During the winter, the sun never rises this far north; sea ice covers the landscape, and temperatures can drop to 60°F below zero (-51°C). But snowy owls are able to survive thanks to their layers of feathers. Even their feet are covered with feathers ... like a pair of fluffy slippers! To help keep them protected from the frigid Arctic climate, their feathers are super thick—so thick that the extra weight helps earn them the title of America's heaviest owl.

Snowy owls spend most of their time in open, barren stretches of the Arctic called tundra. They perch on the ground or on fenceposts, waiting to ambush their prey. The owls are skilled hunters with keen eyesight and hearing, senses that help them find a meal when it's covered by thick vegetation or even hiding under snow. Small rodents called lemmings are a snowy owl's favorite food, and a single owl can eat more than 1,600 of them in a year. But if lemmings aren't available, snowy owls will feast on other critters, including arctic hares, mice, and ducks.

Sometimes, snowy owls migrate to Canada, the northern United States, Europe, and Asia, in the summer in pursuit of food. But often, they remain in their Arctic breeding grounds all year-round.

FAMILY: Strigidae

OTHER COMMON NAMES: arctic owl

SCIENTIFIC NAME: *Bubo scandiacus*

SIZE: 28 inches (71 cm) long, with a wingspan up to 58 inches (147 cm), weighing up to 6.5 pounds (2.9 kg)

FOOD: lemmings and voles

SOCIAL NETWORK: often pairs for life

HABITAT: open tundra, near edge of polar seas

RANGE: Arctic regions in North America and Eurasia

Bet You Didn't Know!

Female and male snowy owls pair up to raise their owlets. The female sits on her nest to keep the eggs warm until they hatch about a month later. The male hunts all the time to find enough lemmings for himself, the owlets, and their mother. By the time the owlets are five to seven weeks old, they will be hunting on their own.

Because the Arctic sun never sets, snowy owls can hunt during the day. That makes them different from most owls, which hunt only at night.

A snowy owl takes flight in Canada.

185

Weddell seals' underwater calls are so loud that they can be heard by a person above the ice.

A Weddell seal mother with her pup beneath an ice floe

INTELLIGENT INSULATION:
WEDDELL SEAL

No seal lives farther south than the Weddell seal. These carnivores spend most of their time below the ice of their Antarctic home, hunting for prey in chilly water. To catch their favorite foods of fish, squid, octopus, and prawns, these marine mammals sport some incredible swimming skills: They can stay underwater for 45 minutes at a time and dive to depths of 2,360 feet (720 m).

That deep diving is a smart strategy: By approaching their prey from below, the seal's intended meals are silhouetted against the bright ice above, making them easy to spot. Weddell seals have also been known to blow air into cracks in the ice, scaring out small fish that are hiding inside—sending them straight into the seal's mouth.

It's extremely cold this far underwater. Good thing Weddell seals have a built-in wet suit: A thick layer of fat called blubber traps heat inside their bodies to keep them warm. Weddell seals have so much blubber that up to 40 percent of their bodies are fat! It works so well at warming them up that when the seals come out of the water on a sunny day, their bodies will often melt the snow and ice around them.

Weddell seals may live under the ice, but they are still mammals that have to breathe air. During winter, cracks in the ice can freeze closed while the seals are hunting. So the animals use their sharp canine teeth to chisel open new breathing holes. They're able to recall the location of these holes and navigate to them, even in the darkness of the Antarctic winter.

FAMILY: Phocidae

SCIENTIFIC NAME: *Leptonychotes weddellii*

SIZE: 10 feet (3 m) long, 1,200 pounds (544 kg)

FOOD: fish, crustaceans, octopuses, and other marine animals

SOCIAL NETWORK: live in groups called pods

HABITAT: Antarctic waters

RANGE: all around the coastal waters of Antarctica

A Weddell seal rests on sea ice.

HEAT-TRAPPER: ADÉLIE PENGUIN

In September and October—springtime in Antarctica—Adélie penguins gather by the thousands on the rocky shore in huge groups called colonies. They build nests with rocks—the only material available in their barren home—and then the female lays two eggs inside.

The penguins are very good parents. The pair takes turns making sure the eggs keep warm, one remaining behind to cover the nest while the other heads out to sea to feast. Then they switch, giving the other penguin in the pair a chance to eat. When the eggs hatch into fluffy chicks, in December, the penguins keep up their team parenting, taking turns caring for the youngsters until they're about three weeks old. Then, the chicks are old enough to be left without a guardian. Large numbers of them gather together for safety in groups called crèches.

By March, the chicks are about nine weeks old and their baby feathers have been replaced by adult ones. Ready to hunt on their own, they plunge into the chilly Antarctic water for the first time. Adélie penguins are swift swimmers, with torpedo-shaped bodies that help them speed through the water. They use their flipper-like wings not for flying but to help propel themselves though the water. These penguins have been known to travel 185 miles (298 km) round-trip to hunt down a meal.

Like many birds in cold climates, these penguins have feathers that repel water. On land, these black-and-white birds fluff their feathers to trap heat and stay warm. But what really keeps them warm is a layer of fat just beneath their skin. In fact, Adélie penguins are so well-built for the cold that they overheat if temperatures get close to the freezing mark of 32°F (0°C)!

FAMILY: Spheniscidae

SCIENTIFIC NAME: *Pygoscelis adeliae*

SIZE: up to 27.5 inches (70 cm)

FOOD: krill, but also fish and squid

SOCIAL NETWORK: live in colonies during breeding season in the spring

HABITAT: islands in summer, ice pack in winter

RANGE: Antarctic continent and nearby islands

An Adélie penguin feeds its newly hatched chick.

Adélie penguins have been spotted stealing rocks from their neighbors' nests.

Bet You Didn't Know!

Birds have special adaptations to help them survive storms. When many birds groom themselves, they distribute oil from glands in their skin all over their feathers to waterproof themselves.

CHAPTER 10
LIFE IN THE TEMPERATE ZONE

Warm summers, brisk autumns, snowy winters, and rainy springs: This is the weather of the temperate zone, which lies between Earth's tropical and polar regions. This location makes the temperate zone neither hot nor cold but somewhere in between. These areas are known for their moderate weather and lack of extreme temperature swings, but that doesn't mean conditions are the same from day to day: Many regions within the temperate zone experience four very different seasons. They can be pelted by hurricanes, swelter in a heat wave, or be buried under snow. The diverse group of people and animals that live here have adapted to weather that is constantly changing.

About 50 percent of the world's population lives within 62 miles (100 km) of the ocean.

192

CLIMATE IN THE TEMPERATE ZONE

The temperate zone lies between 30° and 60° latitude in both the Northern and Southern Hemispheres. Much of the United States, Europe, and the southern half of South America fall within this climate. In its mild conditions, plants and animals flourish. And many people consider it some of the world's best weather.

Because of their location on the globe, the temperate zone doesn't receive the intense sunlight the Equator gets. It also doesn't receive sunlight at an extreme angle, like the poles do. So the seasonal weather changes in the temperate zone fall in between these extremes.

There are two types of temperate climates: maritime and continental. Maritime climates occur in places close to the ocean. Here, the temperature doesn't change too much: That's because water holds a lot of heat—much more than soil or rock does—and it holds on to the heat long after the nearby land has cooled down. So that vast amount of heat-holding water keeps the temperature from changing too much throughout the year. The United Kingdom is one place with a maritime climate. Here, temperatures only vary by about 50°F (27.7°C) throughout the year.

Regions with continental climates are away from the coast, in the interior of a landmass. Without the ocean nearby to moderate temperatures, these regions have hot summers and colder winters. The northern United States is an example of a continental climate, where the temperature can range by as much as 104°F (57°C) from summer to winter.

WHY DOES EARTH HAVE SEASONS?

Seasons happen because Earth is tilted as it orbits around the sun. Sometimes, its top leans towards the sunlight. That makes it summer in the Northern Hemisphere, or the top half of Earth. It's also why the sun never sets in the North Pole during the summer. Other times, Earth's top leans away from the sun. That's what causes winter in the Northern Hemisphere and summer in the Southern Hemisphere (or bottom half of Earth), which is exposed to more direct sunlight during those times. The temperate zone's location on the globe means that the amount of sunlight is constantly changing throughout the year, creating the four seasons.

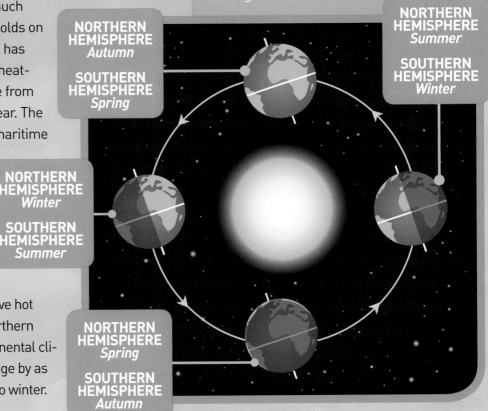

NORTHERN HEMISPHERE
Autumn
SOUTHERN HEMISPHERE
Spring

NORTHERN HEMISPHERE
Summer
SOUTHERN HEMISPHERE
Winter

NORTHERN HEMISPHERE
Winter
SOUTHERN HEMISPHERE
Summer

NORTHERN HEMISPHERE
Spring
SOUTHERN HEMISPHERE
Autumn

HIKING THE APPALACHIAN TRAIL

APPALACHIAN TRAIL →

In May 1955, a 67-year-old grandmother named Emma Gatewood headed out the door, telling her children that she was "going for a hike in the woods."

But she left out an important detail: That "hike in the woods" was actually the Appalachian Trail, a route that snakes from the temperate rainforests of northern Georgia to the alpine tundra of northern Maine, U.S.A. And Gatewood intended to be the first woman to complete it solo.

At about 2,200 miles (3,500 km) long, the Appalachian Trail is the longest hiking-only footpath in the world. Every year, thousands of people set out to make it the entire distance. But only one in four get all the way to the trail's end: Mount Katahdin in Maine. It's not just the distance that makes the Appalachian Trail challenging: It's the weather.

The trail follows the spine of one of the oldest mountain chains on Earth. Someone hiking north from Georgia to Maine—as Gatewood did—climbs an incredible 464,500 vertical feet (141,580 m). At the higher elevations, temperatures can dip to near-freezing in mid-summer, even in mild areas like Tennessee. Humid air rising up the slopes can erupt into thunderstorms with little warning. And for hikers exposed on mountain ridges, lightning can be a serious danger. If they survive the lightning, they still have to deal with rain—more than 100 inches (254 cm) can pour down on the highest peaks of the temperate rainforest of the Blue Ridge Mountains in northern Georgia and southwest North Carolina.

The heat can be brutal, too: The trail passes through Harper's Ferry, West Virginia, where the record high temperature is 107°F (42°C). As hikers make their way north, the temperatures drop. Mount Washington, in New Hampshire, is known as the "home of the world's worst weather." Here, spring snowstorms are common, and winds once gusted as high as 231 miles an hour (372 km/h).

It was into these conditions that Grandma Gatewood—sporting sneakers and carrying a home-made backpack—set off. Without even a sleeping bag, a tent, a compass, or a map, she walked day after day, week after week. On a cold and windy September 25, 1955, with aching muscles and swollen feet, Gatewood took the last few steps to the top of the final hurdle, Mount Katahdin. She signed her name in the register and sang "America the Beautiful." Five months and multiple pairs of canvas sneakers later, she had completed her goal.

But Gatewood didn't stop after becoming the first woman to hike the Appalachian Trail alone. Two years later, she did it again—this time, she said, so she could enjoy it. That made her the first person, male or female, to tackle the trail twice. In 1964, she hiked the trail a third time, in sections. Today, Grandma Gatewood is a hero to everyone who braves the Appalachian Trail's distance and harsh weather, reminding them that if a 67-year-old

mother of 11 and grandmother of 23 could do it, maybe they can, too.

OPPOSITE: Emma "Grandma" Gatewood hiking the Appalachian Trail

TOP: On the trail from May to September, Gatewood wore out six pairs of sneakers in 146 days.

ABOVE: Gatewood in 1942, before her history-making journey

PEOPLE IN THE TEMPERATE ZONE

Ancient humans thrived in the temperate zone. More than 8,000 years ago, an early civilization emerged in Mesopotamia—an area of southwest Asia located in modern-day Iraq, Syria, and parts of Iran and Turkey that's often called "the cradle of civilization." Today, the area has a semidesert climate. But thousands of years ago, the land was much wetter than it is today.

Summers in ancient Mesopotamia were hot, with temperatures that could exceed 110°F (43°C) in some areas. But winters were cool and rainy. Mesopotamia means "between two rivers," because the area was located in a valley between the Tigris and Euphrates Rivers. Every year, heavy rains caused the rivers to flood their banks, covering the valley between in a rich layer of soil called silt. Ancient people found that these conditions were perfect for growing plants. Slowly, people ended their hunter-gatherer lifestyles and grouped together to farm crops for the first time.

Today, people live in temperate areas all over the world. From the Mediterranean coast to the grasslands of Central Asia to the mountains of North America, humans have settled into the many different environments of the temperate zone. Although the temperate zone is the mildest on Earth, that doesn't mean it's always easy to survive. The changes between seasons can be dramatic, and the areas within the temperate zone can vary greatly from place to place. To make a life there, humans have had to change their behaviors—and even their bodies!

AMAZING ADAPTATIONS

Not all temperate areas are gentle places to live. In many places around the world, humans have made their homes in high mountain ranges. Here, the air pressure is low; as a result, the air is low in oxygen. People who travel to high altitudes can suffer from hypoxia, also called mountain sickness—a condition that can cause headaches, vomiting, weakness, and impaired thinking. But people throughout the world native to high-altitude areas don't suffer from hypoxia. They have evolved different methods for dealing with their sky-high lifestyle.

In Tibet, the highest region on Earth (below), they increase their oxygen by taking more breaths per minute. They also have larger blood vessels that help deliver oxygen more effectively throughout their bodies. In the Andes Mountains of South America, people breathe at the same rate as people at sea level, but their blood has an increased amount of hemoglobin. Hemoglobin is a substance in red blood cells that carries oxygen through the system. Extra hemoglobin in the blood brings more oxygen through the body, allowing mountain people to breathe freely in places where others would be gasping for air.

The vast majority of Earth's humans live within the temperate zone.

AT HOME IN THE TEMPERATE ZONE

What is **EVERYDAY LIFE** like for people in the temperate zone?

Bet You Didn't Know!

SNOWED IN

When winter hits, temperatures turn cold. In many places in the temperate zone, freezing winds bring in snow and ice. These conditions can make being outside uncomfortable, or even dangerous, for many people. They have to heat their homes and wear layers of thick clothing to keep warm. But many go outside anyway, enjoying the cold season with such snow sports as skiing, skating, and snowboarding. For Earth's plants and animals, winter is about surviving until spring comes. Many trees lose their leaves entirely and stay dormant, or inactive. Some animals hibernate to wait out the winter, and others migrate to warmer climates. The shortest day of the year for the Northern Hemisphere, the winter solstice, falls in late December. Since it signals that winter's halfway mark has been reached, and the days will begin to grow longer from then on, it is a time of celebration in many parts of the world.

The shades of orange, yellow, and red that leaves "turn" in the fall were actually there all along! All green plants contain chemicals called carotenoids, which give many fruits and veggies their color (think tomatoes and carrots). In leaves, these colors are concealed beneath the green pigment of chlorophyll for much of the year. When the chlorophyll breaks down—ta-da!—we get fall foliage.

You know that Earth is tilted, but have you ever wondered why? Experts believe Earth collided with a massive object in space billions of years ago, when our planet was still forming, and that this crash knocked it off-kilter.

RAINY DAYS

After the long winter's chill, the weather begins to warm up. Spring can bring with it lots of rain, which means people don waterproof coats and boots before they go outside. All that rainfall, along with melting snow, can cause problematic flooding along waterways such as rivers. But although it can be inconvenient for humans, March and April's rainfall is what makes seeds take root and plants begin to grow. That vegetation provides food for animals, so many wake up from hibernation or migrate back from warmer climates—often with their newborn babies alongside them!

FUN IN THE SUN

Late June marks the beginning of the season. It's the summer solstice, the day Earth's Northern Hemisphere is tilted closest toward the sun. During the summer, temperatures rise to the warmest they will be all year. Temperature spikes can cause heat waves that mean trouble for people, animals, and plants. But the warm temperatures also help crops that were planted in the spring spend this season growing. In places with a lot of agriculture, such as the U.S. Midwest, farmers spend summer working in the fields. The sun sets late, and many people spend the long summer days outside, swimming, hiking, and enjoying the warm weather.

HARVEST TIME

When autumn comes, the days start to get shorter as the Northern Hemisphere begins to tilt away from the sun. Temperatures start to drop, prompting humans to find their jackets and some trees, such as sycamore and birch, to lose their leaves. As the amount of daylight decreases, photosynthesis begins to diminish and the trees slow down their production of chlorophyll, the chemical that helps plants make food from sunlight and gives leaves their green color. As chlorophyll gradually disappears, leaves turn shades of red, orange, and yellow. Some animals begin to grow the thick coats that will help them survive the winter's chill. Others spend their days eating to gain weight in preparation for hibernation. Both they and humans have a bounty of food to eat, because autumn is the harvest season—the time when crops planted in the spring are ready to eat.

WHY IS THE SKY BLUE?

After a few days of gloomy weather, a glimpse of bright blue sky peeking through the clouds is a welcome sight. But have you ever stopped to wonder what gives the sky its brilliant color? Why is it blue instead of pink, or yellow, or any other color?

Light from the sun looks white. But it's actually made up of all the colors of the rainbow mixed together. If you shine sunlight through a specially shaped crystal called a prism, you can watch as the white light is separated into all its individual colors: red, orange, yellow, green, blue, and violet.

As the sun's light beams all the way through space to Earth, it has to pass through the atmosphere, which is made of up of tiny molecules of oxygen, nitrogen, and other elements. There are also molecules of other substances up there, like dust, smoke, and haze.

As light moves, it travels in waves. Some of these waves are short and choppy, and other waves are long and lazy. Light toward the red end of the spectrum has lower energy and travels in long waves, while light toward the blue end of the spectrum has higher energy and travels in short waves. As these waves of light move through the atmosphere, they sometimes hit molecules in the atmosphere and bounce off course. This is called "scattering."

Because blue light ping-pongs back and forth in short, high-energy waves, it's more likely to hit particles in the atmosphere and scatter. It bounces around, jumping from particle to particle before it finally reaches your eye. That means there is a lot of blue light coming at your eyes from all directions. There's so much blue light that it blots out the light coming from the stars, which is there even during the day. And that's what makes the sky look blue.

It's Earth's atmosphere that causes the sky to be blue. Mercury, a planet that has no real atmosphere, has colorless skies.

Hot-air balloons take flight at the 2014 Albuquerque International Balloon Fiesta, in New Mexico, U.S.A.

ANIMALS IN THE TEMPERATE ZONE

Animals crawl, hop, bounce, and pounce all over Earth's temperate zone. These areas are friendly places for life—until winter hits. Then, temperatures drop, and there isn't much food to go around. So animals have adapted different methods for surviving until spring, when the weather warms, plants sprout, and food is plentiful again.

Some creatures simply wait out the winter months. But others enter a sleeplike state of inactivity in which their lungs, hearts, and brains slow down and their body temperatures drop. In mammals, this is called hibernation—a way for them to conserve their energy. Groundhogs' body temperatures drop to about 41°F (5°C) for about a week at a time. Then, they'll wake up for a few days, eat food they have stored, and relieve themselves. They'll repeat this pattern between 12 and 20 times over the winter.

Unlike warm-blooded animals, cold-blooded creatures rely on the heat of the sun to warm their bodies. When temperatures drop for the winter, it puts many of them in danger of freezing. So like their furry cousins, many reptiles and amphibians enter an inactive state during the winter. For these cold-blooded animals, it's called brumation.

Other animals flee the region during the cold winter months, escaping to a warmer area in an act called migration. Southern right whales, for example, spend their summers eating in the cold Antarctic waters. In the winter, they migrate to temperate areas along the coasts of Chile and Argentina to breed. Swallows (far right) are some of the world's most famous migrators. European swallows travel 200 miles (322 km) a day to spend the cold season in Africa south of the Sahara. That's a long way to go to escape winter!

Bet You Didn't Know!

Hibernation doesn't only happen in colder regions. Animals in the tropics, such as the fat-tailed dwarf lemur of Madagascar, will hibernate during the dry season. In the dry bush of Australia, echidnas (also known as spiny anteaters) have been observed to enter a state of torpor after wildfires, saving their energy until the return of one of their main food sources: ants.

ECHIDNA

Animals in the temperate zone live in a variety of ecosystems, including prairie, mountain, forest, and coastal habitats.

SLOWING DOWN TO SURVIVE:
BROWN BEAR

Sleeping away the long, dark days of winter might sound like a pretty good idea.

But the reality of it would be challenging: Not long after you started snoozing, your belly would start to rumble with hunger, your heart would get tired, your muscles would begin to weaken—and you'd definitely need to go to the bathroom! But for a brown bear, none of this is a problem.

In areas where winters are cold, brown bears spend the fall season in a marathon eating session. They pack on the pounds so that they can survive off their fat stores for the four to seven months they're about to spend hibernating. Brown bears can gain 30 pounds (14 kg) per week during this season! When the cold hits, fattened bears waddle into dens they find among rocks or dig among tree roots.

Brown bear cubs are born during the winter. The mother briefly comes out of hibernation to give birth, then returns to her sleeplike state. The cubs spend the winter nursing, warm and protected inside the den. When the weather warms up in April or May, the little bears are big enough to leave the den and explore the forest with their mother.

When most people think of hibernation, they think of bears. But scientists don't consider bears to be "true" hibernators like ground squirrels or chipmunks, whose body temperature drops to almost freezing while they hibernate. In comparison, bears' body temperature drops by only about 10.8°F (6°C). But their metabolism, or energy their body uses, drops by 75 percent. To survive on barely any fuel, bears' hearts beat only about four times per minute. And, unlike any other mammal, bears don't wake up to go to the bathroom all winter.

FAMILY: Ursidae

OTHER COMMON NAMES: In North America, some are called grizzly bears.

SCIENTIFIC NAME: *Ursus arctos*

SIZE: up to 700 pounds (318 kg)

FOOD: grasses, roots, berries, insects, fish, mammals, and carrion

HABITAT: temperate forest

RANGE: North America, Europe, and Asia

Bet You Didn't Know!

Some animals take hibernation to the extreme! When winter comes, the bodies of wood frogs slowly freeze. Their hearts stop beating, their organs stop working, and their blood turns to ice. But the frogs don't die. When spring comes, they defrost, their bodies start up again, and they hop away!

THEY COME OUT AT NIGHT

For humans, night is a time to curl up and sleep. But whether it's to avoid the heat of the day or search for food under the protective cover of darkness, many of the world's creatures emerge at night instead.

LITTLE BROWN BAT

There's no nocturnal creature better known than the bat. The only mammals capable of flight, little brown bats head out at night to hunt down insects, which thrive in the mild climate of the temperate zone. To do it, bats rely on a sixth sense: echolocation, the ability to sense what's around them by emitting high-pitched calls and listening to how they bounce off their surroundings. Bats are expert hunters—one can eat up to 1,000 mosquitoes in a single hour!

PORCUPINE

These prickly rodents live in temperate and tropical habitats in parts of Asia, southern Europe, Africa, and North and South America. Their coats of sharp spines, or quills, act like natural armor, making any predator think twice before they try to make a meal out of this barbed rodent. They snooze during the heat of the day and emerge at night to forage for nuts, bark, seeds, leaves, and fruit.

Porcupines are sometimes called "porkies" or "quill pigs."

EUROPEAN BADGER

The largest land predator in the United Kingdom, the black-and-white badger is less active when temperatures drop in the winter. But it's not a true hibernator, and when the weather is mild enough, it comes out at night to eat, gobbling down everything from vegetables to small mammals. But a badger's favorite food is worms: An adult can slurp up more than 200 of them in a single night!

KOALA

The heat of the Australian sun can be intense. That's why koalas are generally active only at night—if they're active at all, that is! These marsupials sleep for around 14.5 hours a day and spend nearly another five hours resting. But it's not because they're lazy: Koalas' diet of eucalyptus takes a lot of energy to digest.

KIWI

These fluffy brown birds, native to New Zealand, have nostrils located at the tips of their bills—the better to sniff out the worms, grubs, and other invertebrates they hunt for at night. Today, kiwis have no natural predators on their island home. But experts believe that they may have evolved their nocturnal habit to avoid competition with the giant moa, a now-extinct flightless bird that could grow as tall as 12 feet (3.6 m). Now, many species of kiwi are at risk of extinction, too, and warmer temperatures due to climate change are stressing them further.

MARVELOUS MIGRATOR:
MONARCH BUTTERFLY

Many animals travel to spend the winter season in a warmer climate. But perhaps the planet's most marvelous migrator is the black-and-orange monarch butterfly.

Each fall, as temperatures begin to drop, monarch butterflies take to the sky by the millions. Powered only by their delicate wings, these insects flap farther than many much sturdier migrators, traveling up to 3,000 miles (4,828 km) from their summer breeding grounds in the northeastern United States and Canada to their wintering grounds in southwestern Mexico.

Such an epic journey for such a fragile creature is amazing enough. But there's something even more incredible about monarch migration: Unlike birds or wildebeest, which embark on similar journeys each year, individual butterflies don't live long enough to make the whole trip. Instead, it takes several generations of butterflies to complete the journey. Yet without a previous trip or an experienced companion to guide them, monarchs manage to follow the same route as their great-grandparents— sometimes even returning to the same tree! How the monarchs know when to leave and where to go is a mystery scientists are still trying to solve.

FAMILY: Nymphalidae

OTHER COMMON NAMES: Monarch

SCIENTIFIC NAME: *Danaus plexippus plexippus*

SIZE: wingspan of 3.5 to 4 inches (8.9–10.2 cm)

FOOD: The caterpillars eat only milkweed plants; the butterflies eat nectar.

HABITAT: a range from marshes to mountains

RANGE: North America

Bet You Didn't Know!

Monarchs, like most butterflies, are highly sensitive to the weather and climate. They rely on changes in temperature to cue them when to reproduce, migrate, and hibernate.

Foxes, coyotes, lynx, and some birds of prey hunt the snowshoe hare for food.

HIDING IN PLAIN SIGHT:
SNOWSHOE HARE

The snowshoe hare—named for its large, furry feet—takes a cautious hop across the powdery snowfall, its nose twitching.

It is searching out its nighttime snack of shrubs, grasses, and plants, while keeping an eye out for the many predators who'd love to make a meal of it, including the lynx, fox, and coyote. But thanks to its superwhite fur, the hare is hard to spot against the snow!

Snowshoe hares live in forest habitats in North America, from as far south as Virginia and New Mexico to as far north as the coast of the Arctic. In the northern parts of their range, their white coats help blend them into the winter scenery. But this furry critter has another trick up its sleeve: When the weather warms and the snow melts each spring, it switches out its white coat for a brown one.

It takes about 10 weeks for snowshoe hares to change their coat color. They're one of dozens of species living in temperate climates around the globe—including stoats (a type of weasel) and birds called ptarmigans—that have this ability. Scientists have marveled at this feat for centuries. But now they've got a new reason to be interested: Climate change is melting the yearly snow faster and earlier, turning places that were once blanketed in white browner every year. If the hares aren't able to adjust to the changing climate—shedding their winter coats sooner in the spring and delaying their change from brown to white in the fall, for example—they could lose their ability to hide in plain sight, making them easier for predators to see. Like many species facing climate change, their survival could hinge on their ability to adapt with a changing planet.

FAMILY: Leporidae

OTHER COMMON NAMES: varying hare, snowshoe rabbit

SCIENTIFIC NAME: *Lepus americanus*

SIZE: 2 to 4 pounds (0.9–1.8 kg)

FOOD: plants

HABITAT: temperate and boreal forests

RANGE: North America

Bet You Didn't Know!

In 2018, scientists reported that some snowshoe hares were keeping their brown summer coats year-round. They analyzed the animals' genes and determined that the hares had mated with another species, the black-tailed jackrabbit, that doesn't change its coat color. As a result, they lost their ability to turn white with the winter!

SUPERSIZE SUN-SEEKER: AMERICAN ALLIGATOR

During the warm months, alligators can be seen all over the waterways of the southeastern United States. These cold-blooded animals rely on the heat of the sun to warm their bodies. So what do alligators in the temperate zone do during the winter?

To survive the changing seasons, alligators brumate, entering a state similar to hibernation. Some burrow in lairs along the banks of a river or lake, while others lie at the bottom of a swamp. When the sun shines on them, the alligators become active, using this time to hunt. At night, the water cools, and the alligators' breathing and metabolism temporarily slow down. Brumation can last for just a night, until the daylight warms Earth again, or it can last for the entire season. Alligators can even survive below-freezing temperatures this way: Right before the surface of the water freezes, they will stick their snouts out of the water so they can continue breathing. Then, they brumate the winter away, becoming alert again when the ice melts.

Alligators have fine-tuned their survival strategies over a very long time. They're one of the few species on Earth that has remained almost unchanged for 150 million years. They walked Earth with the dinosaurs, then managed to survive the massive extinction that killed off most of the dinosaurs 65 million years ago. Though they are clumsy on land, alligators are highly adapted to life in the water, where they use their massive jaws and strong swimming skills to hunt anything they can grab, including fish, turtles, snakes, and small mammals.

FAMILY: Alligatoridae

SCIENTIFIC NAME: *Alligator mississippiensis*

SIZE: up to 15 feet (4.6 m)

FOOD: all kinds of animals, including invertebrates, fish, turtles, snakes, birds, amphibians, and mammals

HABITAT: rivers, lakes, swamps, and marshes

RANGE: the southeastern United States

CROCODILE

ALLIGATOR

Bet You Didn't Know!

The Everglades, in Florida, U.S.A., is the only place on Earth where alligators and crocodiles live together. These two remarkable reptiles are often confused for each other, but there are two sure ways to tell them apart: snouts and smiles! Alligators have short, rounded snouts; crocs have longer, pointier ones. When an alligator closes its mouth, you won't see any of its teeth. But when a croc shuts its mouth, its back teeth stick up over its top lip.

A group of alligators is called a congregation.

Red foxes use their thick, furry tails like blankets to stay warm in cold weather.

SNOW-STALKER:
RED FOX

The red fox stands on the snow, listening intently. Her ears pricked forward, she tilts her head back and forth. Then suddenly, she gathers herself, pounces high in the air, and dives into the snowbank headfirst. When she emerges, she's holding a mouse in her jaws. Dinnertime!

In fables, foxes are intelligent creatures, always outsmarting the rest of the animals. And the truth isn't far off. Red foxes have made their home nearly worldwide in temperate climates including forests, mountains, and grasslands, and desert climates, too. These solitary hunters eat what they can find, from vegetables to fish to worms. Their ability to adapt wherever they go has earned them their reputation for craft and cunning.

Red foxes' wintertime hunting habits are one example. When snow is deep, prey is hidden underneath, meaning many animals go hungry. Red foxes, however, can hear low-frequency sounds—even those of small mammals scampering under three feet (1 m) of snow—extremely well. But they don't owe the trick to hearing alone. In 2010, scientists discovered that nearly all of the time, foxes' snow dives are successful only if the animals are facing northeast or the opposite direction, southwest. Experts suspect that's because they are able to sense Earth's magnetic field. They think foxes use the magnetic field as a kind of "rangefinder" that helps them estimate the distance to their prey under the snow and plot their pounce trajectory. Many animals, including sharks and cows, can sense Earth's magnetic field. But if scientists are correct, the red fox is the only animal known to use it for hunting. Now that's a nifty seasonal survival strategy!

FAMILY: Canidae

SCIENTIFIC NAME: *Vulpes vulpes*

SIZE: 6.5 to 24 pounds (3–11 kg)

FOOD: nearly anything, from plants to garbage left by humans

HABITAT: many habitats, including forests, grasslands, mountains, and deserts

RANGE: across the Northern Hemisphere

A red fox senses something scurrying beneath the icy blanket of snow ...

... and dives head-first into the snow to retrieve its dinner.

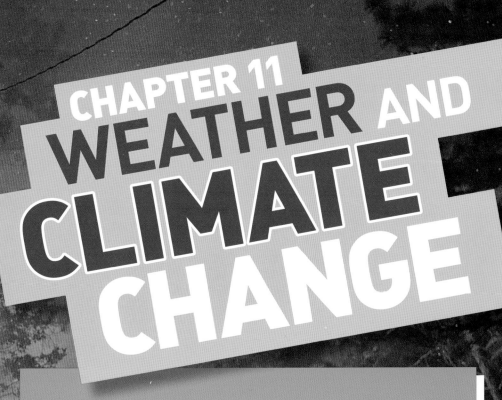

CHAPTER 11
WEATHER AND CLIMATE CHANGE

The world is getting warmer. Scientists predict that over the next century, Earth will warm more than 20 times faster than it has ever warmed over the past two million years. They fear that this rapidly changing climate could make Earth's weather more extreme: worsening droughts in some areas, causing floods in others, and intensifying storms and hurricanes. Both people and animals are already beginning to deal with the weather effects of a changing climate. What does the forecast of the future hold?

In April 2014, Wichita, Kansas, U.S.A., experienced a temperature drop of 50°F (27.7°C) between 1:00 p.m. on a Sunday and 8:00 a.m. on a Monday. Sudden fluctuations in weather, including hot days to cold, have been linked to global warming.

WARMING WORLD

Everyone knows the weather is always changing. It can be below freezing one day and warm enough for short sleeves the next! So what's the big deal about a changing climate?

Remember that climate and weather aren't the same thing. While weather refers to short-term conditions of the atmosphere in a particular place, climate is the average weather in that particular place over an extended amount of time. So when people talk about climate change, they mean long-term changes across the whole planet over a long period. And the reason that experts are concerned about it is that Earth's global climate is warming. The average temperature of the planet's surface has risen about 1.62°F (0.9°C) since the late 19th century.

That might not seem like a huge increase. After all, if the temperature outside changed by that much right now, you would barely notice! But what's alarming to experts is how fast the temperature has changed.

Right now, the planet is warming about 10 times faster than experts would expect it to based on its history of temperature changes. Most of the planet's warming has occurred in the past few decades, and the warmest years ever recorded have all happened since 2010. Nearly every year, new records are set for the hottest months ever documented. As the temperature climbs, glaciers are melting, sea levels are rising, and forests are dying. And the extra heat is changing how weather moves around the planet, too. That is concerning for the living things that depend on the planet—including humans.

HOW DID THIS HAPPEN?

Starting in about 1750, human society went through a major shift. Before that, most people on Earth farmed their own food and made their own tools and supplies by hand. But then, new machines were invented for manufacturing goods and transporting them all over the world. They were powered by burning fossil fuels, such as coal, oil, and gas. This shift, called the industrial revolution, shaped the modern world and helped people survive with less struggle. But now, scientists know the burning of fossil fuels releases gases into the atmosphere. These gases act like an invisible blanket, holding in heat from the sun and causing Earth to warm up. This is called the greenhouse effect. Other human activities, like farming and deforestation, contribute to the planet's warming temperature, too.

CHANGING CLIMATE, CHANGING PLANET

In a sense, climate change is nothing new: Over the billions of years that Earth has existed, its temperature has risen and dropped many times. But the pattern of climate change happening now is very different from what has occurred in the past.

For example, during the Paleocene and Eocene epochs (periods of time), about 66 to 34 million years ago, things were very warm. There were no ice caps at the poles, and there were palm trees and crocodiles in what is now the frigid Arctic. During the Precambrian eon, about 700 million years ago, Earth got so cold that scientists believe it may have been entirely covered in ice from the poles to the tropics, like a giant snowball.

But these warm periods, called interglacials, and cold periods, called ice ages, normally occur in cycles that take 100,000 years to complete. In the past, they were triggered by small increases in the amount of sunlight reaching Earth's surface, and then amplified as the warming temperatures caused the oceans to release large amounts of carbon dioxide. The current period of climate change is happening at a much faster rate. Scientists think the planet is probably warming faster than it has at any comparable point over the past million years.

Warmer temperatures aren't the only result of climate change; it has many side effects that are altering the planet. For one, Earth's ice is melting: The Greenland ice sheet has lost an average of 281 billion tons (253 billion t) of ice per year between 1993 and 2016, while the Antarctic ice sheet has lost about 119 billion tons (108 billion t) over the same time period. Glaciers in the Alps, Himalaya, Andes, Rockies, and other areas around the world are shrinking. That melting, plus the increased ocean temperatures, has caused the global sea level to rise by about 4 to 8 inches (10–20 cm) over the past 100 years. And with these changes, the planet's weather has begun to change, too.

HOW DO WE KNOW?

Humans have been keeping accurate weather records across the entire globe since only about 1880. So how do we know the current pattern of climate change is something out of the ordinary?

To peek into the past and see that Earth's climate has shifted over its history, scientists have had to get creative. One way they do it is by drilling into glacier ice to extract ice cores—samples of ice from deep down that can date back to when the glacier was first formed. Trapped inside the ice are bits of whatever was floating around in the atmosphere at that point in Earth's past, including air bubbles, ash from volcanic eruptions, and soot from forest fires, giving scientists clues about what the climate was like back then. Climate scientists also look at tree rings, a pattern of circles inside a tree's trunk made during a tree's life. By their color and width, tree rings can show how warm and rainy past years were. By using these sources and others, scientists can get a detailed record of Earth's climate that stretches back thousands of years.

Scientists measure the sea level of the Ross Sea in Antarctica.

If Greenland's ice sheet were to melt completely, the world's sea level would rise by an estimated 20 feet (6 m).

Glacier calving is when ice chunks break off from the edge of a glacier. Here, the Dawes Glacier in Alaska's Tongass National Forest, calves from its 200-foot (61-m)-high face.

AN EXTREME FUTURE

A warmer planet might not sound so bad. It might even be nice if winters weren't quite so cold and everyone could wear their summer clothes a little longer! Unfortunately, rising temperatures don't mean that Earth will have nicer weather. In fact, scientists predict that climate change will make our weather more extreme and unpredictable.

More Heat Waves, Droughts, and Wildfires

As the planet's temperature warms, evaporation increases. This can cause areas of Earth's surface to dry out and heat up, leading to droughts. In 2011, Texas had its hottest summer on record, with many areas experiencing more than 100 days hotter than 100°F (38°C). The hot, dry conditions damaged corn crops, causing food prices to spike. Drought conditions can also worsen wildfires, causing brush to dry out until it turns to tinder: There are five times more fires today than there were in the 1970s.

The Woolsey Fire that raged in California, U.S.A., in late 2018 engulfed tens of thousands of acres of land and destroyed many homes.

More Rainfall and Floods

Because of the increase in evaporation, the amount of water in the atmosphere goes up, too. All that water has to go somewhere, so it comes down as added precipitation. In the U.S. Pacific Northwest, heavy rainfall events have increased by 70 percent over the past six decades. As rainfall increases, so does flooding. Floods caused more than 500,000 deaths worldwide from 1980 to 2009, and experts think their effect will worsen in the future.

In 2009, more than 12 inches (31 cm) of rain fell in 24 hours in the county of Cumbria, England, causing unprecedented flooding.

Snowstorms

Blizzards are a normal part of weather on Earth. But just as warmer temperatures increase the amount of rainfall because a warmer atmosphere leads to more water vapor in the air, they also increase the snowfall during winter storms. Since the 1950s, winter storms have become more frequent and more intense.

In August 2017, Hurricane Harvey caused catastrophic damage and destruction to buildings like this one in Rockport, Texas, U.S.A.

Stronger Hurricanes

Extra heat in the air and the oceans means more energy—the kind of energy that drives storms. Scientists don't yet know if the warming global temperature causes an increase in the number of storms. But they think it might cause storms to intensify, carrying more precipitation with higher wind speeds. At the end of the 20th century, a storm on par with Hurricane Harvey in 2017 was likely to occur once every 100 years, experts said. Now, they think the chance of that kind of storm striking is estimated to be once every 16 years.

ANIMALS AND CLIMATE CHANGE

Shrinking sea ice, warming oceans, and changing weather patterns are already affecting living things all over the planet. Here are a few of the animals that experts fear may be hit hardest by climate change.

Polar Bears

The Arctic is warming faster than anywhere else, causing sea ice there to shrink by 14 percent each decade. Polar bears depend on the sea ice to hunt seals, which they capture when the seals surface for air through breathing holes in the ice. Now, the ice is breaking up sooner in the spring and forming later in the fall, forcing some bears to walk or swim long distances to get to the ice. Over the past 10 years, the population of polar bears in one region, the Beaufort Sea area north of Canada, has declined by 40 percent.

Orangutans

Orangutans are already one of planet Earth's most threatened species: They live in only two places in the wild, the Indonesian island of Sumatra and the island of Borneo, where they face danger of extinction as humans move into and cut down tropical forests. Now experts think these creatures will face serious danger from climate change, too, as altered rainfall patterns create shortages of the fruit and leaves they depend on for food. Facing all these threats, the population of Bornean orangutans shrunk by half between 1999 and 2015.

Sea Turtles

Every year, sea turtles return to the beach where they were born to lay their eggs. And the temperature of the sand is very important: As with many reptiles, it determines whether the baby sea turtles will be male or female. If temperatures are roughly 85°F (29°C), equal amounts of male and female turtles will hatch. But as temperatures increase, the world could see more female turtles hatching—and if there are too many female turtles and not enough males, they can't reproduce, which is bad news for the species' long-term survival. In 2018, scientists reported that in one section of Australian beach along the Great Barrier Reef, more than 99 percent of green sea turtles hatched as female.

Corals

Coral isn't just colorful seafloor decoration: It's a living species. Corals are tiny animals that look like itty-bitty jellyfish. They float in the water until they find a hard place to attach to, such as a coral reef, where they then build shells to live inside. A coral reef is made of about a million of these individual shells stuck together. But corals are very sensitive animals easily stressed by temperature changes of warming oceans. Experts predict that many reefs, including the world's largest, the Great Barrier Reef, will likely not survive if warming trends continue.

SURVIVING IN A CHANGING CLIMATE

Climate change has made planet Earth a tougher place to survive for many species. But for a few creatures, warming conditions have been a benefit. Marmots in one part of Colorado, U.S.A, are a pound (.45 kg) bigger on average than they were 30 years ago, and experts think climate change is the reason. Marmots are furry rodents that emerge from their burrows in spring, hungry after a winter of hibernating. Over about the past 30 years, spring has arrived an average of one day earlier each year. That gives the marmots more time to eat and store extra fat, helping them better survive the winters. But the marmots' success story may only be short-term: Scientists think that as temperatures continue to rise, increased drought conditions will make survival a struggle for these animals.

HUMANS AND CLIMATE CHANGE

A warming planet isn't just a problem for animals. Climate change impacts human life, too. Here are some of the conditions people are beginning to face in a warming world.

Rising Temperatures

Over the past three to four decades, heat waves around the globe have gotten more frequent and more intense. Thirty percent of the world's population is already endangered by deadly heat waves. And the evidence says that the trend will continue as the global temperature climbs. High heat can be deadly, especially for people who are sick or elderly.

Water Supply

Water is Earth's most precious resource. Regions such as Cape Town, South Africa, are already facing dire water shortages. Cape Town, home to four million people, has gotten only about half its average rainfall each year since 2015. And as temperatures around the world continue to climb, experts expect that droughts will intensify. Areas that are already dry, like the southern United States, will likely become drier.

Air Quality

Brown smog sits in the air over many major cities. Smog—also known as ozone pollution, from sources including car exhaust, factory emissions, gasoline, and paints—can be worsened by warmer temperatures, which tend to keep air from moving away from an area. During 2014 to 2016, years that the planet experienced some of its hottest temperatures ever recorded, the number of days with high levels of ozone pollution increased, too. Lower air quality can cause health problems such as heart and respiratory illness, and people with asthma, emphysema, and chronic obstructive pulmonary disease (COPD) are especially susceptible to the dangers of air pollution.

Agriculture and Food

Farmers depend on a hospitable climate to grow crops that the world needs for food. As climate change leads to heat waves, droughts, floods, and more extreme weather events, harvests suffer. In 2011, the worst drought on record hit Mexico and caused the failure of more than two million acres (809,000 ha) of crops.

Disease

Scientists are concerned that global warming is likely to increase the rates of certain diseases such as malaria, dengue fever, and West Nile virus. That's because these diseases are carried by mosquitoes, which thrive in warm, wet environments. As more regions of the world become mosquito friendly, the number of people infected may also increase. Experts are already reporting cases of mosquito-borne disease in areas where they haven't been seen before.

DISAPPEARING PLACES

As the world warms, rising seas and melting glaciers could actually reshape Earth's very landscape. Experts predict that if current climate patterns continue, some places on the planet could be at risk of vanishing entirely.

GLACIER NATIONAL PARK, MONTANA, U.S.A.

More than three million visitors travel to this national park every year to take in the verdant forests, crystal clear lakes, and, of course, the glaciers that give this place its name. But since 1966, warming temperatures have significantly shrunk 39 of the park's glaciers—some by up to 85 percent. Scientists predict that by the end of the century, there will be no ice left at all.

KEY WEST, FLORIDA, U.S.A.

This sunny stretch of Florida coastline is known for its pastel buildings and pristine snorkeling conditions. But rising sea levels put this coastal community at great risk. Experts estimate that the ocean there will rise 15 inches (38 cm) over the next three decades or so. And increasingly dangerous hurricanes, such as Hurricane Irma, which struck in 2017, could devastate the area as it is submerged.

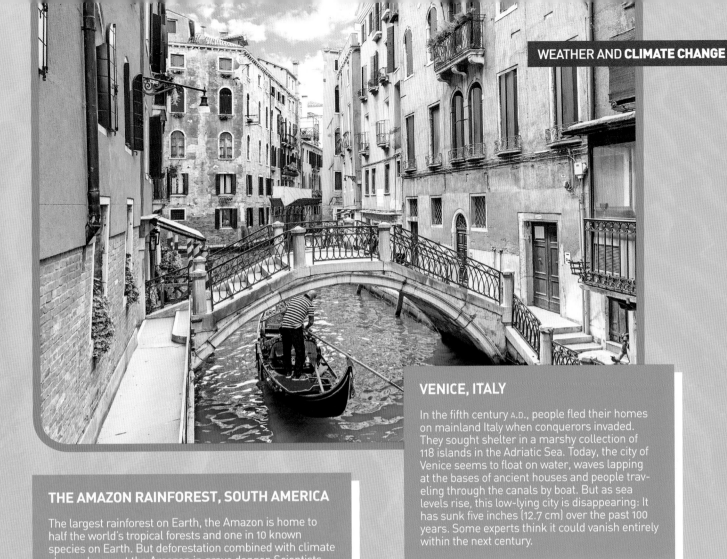

VENICE, ITALY

In the fifth century A.D., people fled their homes on mainland Italy when conquerors invaded. They sought shelter in a marshy collection of 118 islands in the Adriatic Sea. Today, the city of Venice seems to float on water, waves lapping at the bases of ancient houses and people traveling through the canals by boat. But as sea levels rise, this low-lying city is disappearing: It has sunk five inches (12.7 cm) over the past 100 years. Some experts think it could vanish entirely within the next century.

THE AMAZON RAINFOREST, SOUTH AMERICA

The largest rainforest on Earth, the Amazon is home to half the world's tropical forests and one in 10 known species on Earth. But deforestation combined with climate change have put the Amazon in grave danger. Scientists think it could shrink by as much as 85 percent due to climate change over the next century, as lack of rain turns its lush rainforests into savannas.

THE MALDIVES, INDIAN OCEAN

A tropical paradise, the Maldives is a country known for its blue lagoons and vast reefs. In fact, the Maldives is actually built of coral: more than 1,000 coral islands. It's also the lowest-lying country in the world, with most of it sitting only about 3.3 feet (1 m) above the sea's surface. Since the 1950s, sea level in the area has been rising at up to .06 inch (1.5 mm) per year, and increased flooding has forced people to evacuate. Experts think it's likely to be underwater by the end of this century.

STEPPING UP

Climate change is a daunting problem to tackle. But fortunately, people are up to the challenge. Here are stories of humans fighting back—and winning.

New Energy

The machines of the industrial revolution relied on burning fossil fuels for energy, and fossil fuels still provide more than 80 percent of the energy for the industrially developed world. But that's starting to change, with countries pledging to phase out fossil fuels and instead draw their power from renewable resources like wind and water. In 2017, Costa Rica ran for a record 300 days on renewable power. And in a single day—February 22 that same year—Denmark generated enough wind energy to power the electricity needs of the entire country for that day.

Saving Forests

Carbon is a greenhouse gas that warms the planet when it floats in Earth's atmosphere. But plants absorb carbon from the atmosphere and use it to build new leaves, shoots, and roots. In this way, Earth's lush tropical forests are capable of storing huge amounts of carbon, reducing its effects on climate change. The majority of tropical forests are in deep danger

as deforestation shrinks them every year. But in 2017, Indonesia's tropical forest loss dropped by 60 percent. If other countries can follow suit, tropical rainforests can continue to act as the planet's air purifier.

Eager Creatures

Before Europeans moved to North America, there were as many as 400 million beavers inhabiting 60 percent of the continent. It is estimated that by 1900 that number had dropped to just about 100,000. Then, experts started to realize that beavers play a huge role in the health of ecosystems: Their dams and ponds filter out pollution, store water that can be used for farms, and slow floods. Now, conservationists have successfully re-introduced beavers to some of their old habitats. In 2006, one even set up a home in New York's Bronx River for the first time in 200 years.

on for farming was beginning to turn into desert. Farmers decided to take action. They built stone walls to hold in water and transformed rock-hard land into planting areas. Their efforts have made a big difference: Areas that were once brown are turning green again. By 2004, one region, Zinder Valley, had 50 times more trees than it did in 1975.

Future Farming

The Sahel, an arid region on the south border of the Sahara in Africa, spans 3,360 miles (5,400 km) from the Atlantic to the Indian Ocean. Rainfall is rare and droughts are frequent here, and climate change is making both conditions worse. By the mid-20th century, land that generations had relied

WHAT CAN YOU DO?

It might seem like there aren't a lot of ways you can help stop climate change. Many decisions that can make a difference—like choosing an energy-efficient car or installing solar panels on your house—have to wait until adulthood. But there are some things you can do right now. The biggest one is reducing your carbon footprint—the amount of carbon dioxide released into the air because of your energy needs, such as transportation, electricity, food, and clothing. You can turn off TVs, computers, and lights when you don't need them and swap old incandescent light bulbs for energy-efficient ones. You can choose to walk or ride a bike instead of taking a car, or organize a carpool for longer trips. You can carry tap water in a reusable bottle instead of using bottled water. And those are only a few of the ways you can help out planet Earth in the battle against climate change. Can you think of more?

CHAPTER 12
WILD WEATHER

Hold on to your umbrella. If you think sandstorms and lightning are strange, just wait until you turn the page. Planet Earth is home to some truly extreme weather events. From pools of water that dance just out of reach in the dry desert, to rainbows visible only at night, to tornadoes made of fire, this is weather so bizarre it's almost unbelievable.

YOU'RE SEEING THINGS: MIRAGES

Imagine that you're stumbling through the desert, hot and dehydrated, when you spot something ahead in the distance: water. You're saved! Cool and blue, it shimmers invitingly across the hot sand. But when you move toward it, it disappears into thin air. It wasn't water at all. It was a mirage.

You might think someone who spots a mirage is hallucinating. But mirages are actually optical illusions caused by the way light is refracted, or bent through air at different temperatures. Normally, light waves from the sun travel straight through the atmosphere on their way to your eye. But when the ground is very hot and the air is cool, the hot ground can warm a layer of air just above it. When light travels through that layer, it bends from the sky down toward the ground, then back up to your eyes in a U-shaped curve. That makes your eyes perceive an image of the sky on the ground. Because your brain doesn't know the light was bent, it decides this patch of sky must actually be a pool of water. The effect, called an inferior mirage, can be very confusing!

Mirages don't always look like water in the desert. The opposite effect, called a superior mirage, happens when cold air lies closer to the ground with warmer air above it (see diagram). That can cause light to bend downward instead of upward on its way to your eye, making it look like what is on the ground is actually above it, in the sky. Superior mirages can make it look like boats on the horizon are floating above the water. A fata morgana is a complex type of mirage in which distant objects appear extremely distorted. For example, it can make a distant, flat shoreline appear to have tall cliffs and mountains.

GEOGRAPHY GONE WRONG

Mirages were very baffling for early explorers. In 1818, British explorer John Ross was trying to find a Northwest Passage, or a route to the Pacific Ocean through the Arctic Ocean. When he entered Lancaster Sound, a body of water in Canada, he spotted a vast mountain range blocking the sound and decided to turn around. Ross even named the range, calling it the Croker Mountains. But later expeditions showed the range didn't exist; he had been fooled by a superior mirage!

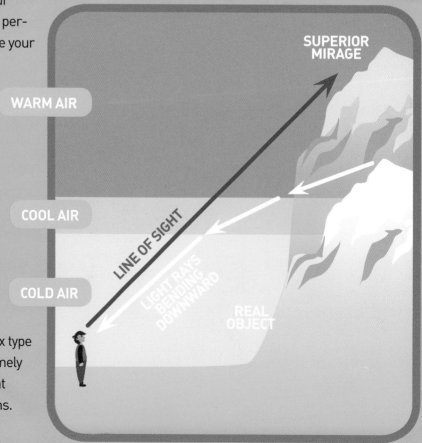

SUPERIOR MIRAGE

WARM AIR

COOL AIR

COLD AIR

LINE OF SIGHT

LIGHT RAYS BENDING DOWNWARD

REAL OBJECT

The best place to spot an inferior mirage is on a hot road.

SPARKS IN THE SKY: ST. ELMO'S FIRE

If you were flying along in an airplane at 37,000 feet (11,278 m) and saw flashes of electricity dancing along the wings, you might think your eyes were playing tricks on you. But you'd just be spotting a rare—yet totally normal—weather phenomenon called St. Elmo's fire.

The event is named after St. Erasmus of Formiae, the patron saint of sailors. That's because sailors were some of the earliest observers of the phenomenon; they often saw the brush-shaped discharges of electricity atop the masts of their ships during thunderstorms at sea. Rather than abandoning ship, they decided the sight was a good omen sent to them from the saint, as it usually signaled that the end of the storm was near.

Like lightning, St. Elmo's fire occurs in nature during thunderstorms, when the ground below the storm is electrically charged and there is high voltage in the air between the cloud and the ground. The voltage breaks apart air molecules and makes them light up, turning them into a glowing gas called plasma. It's the same process that lights up the gas inside neon signs—but St. Elmo's fire happens out in the open.

St. Elmo's fire doesn't just occur on the top of ships and the outside of airplanes (which are built to conduct electricity harmlessly away from the plane's interior). It can also happen on the ground, during intense storms: It's often spotted on the tips of pointed objects such as church towers. There are even a few reports of it being seen on people! As amazing as the effect is, if you ever see St. Elmo's fire, get to safety. Though St. Elmo's fire is not dangerous, it signals that the area is highly charged with electricity, meaning lightning could strike at any moment.

St. Elmo's fire glows blue or violet because of the elements nitrogen and oxygen in our atmosphere.

WEIRD WATER WEATHER

Towering waves, underwater icicles, a mysterious ocean flicker: Sometimes weather conditions are just right to create super strange water effects. Have you ever seen any of these extreme events?

FROZEN FIRE BUBBLES

These icy bubbles beneath the water's surface are enchanting—but don't get too close! They are formed when dead leaves and other matter sink to the bottom of a body of water, where hungry bacteria gobble them up and release methane gas that bubbles upward. In the winter, these bubbles freeze as they near the water's chilly surface. Researchers are concerned that Earth's warming temperature is increasing the amount of methane released through lakes. Scientists are using a brave method to test this idea: poking holes in the ice and setting fire to the gas inside to see what it's made of!

BRINICLES

You might have seen icicles hanging from the eaves of houses after a cold snap. But did you know the same thing can happen underwater? Supercold, salty water trapped in sea ice pushes down through the ice and enters the seawater, which is much warmer. As the "brinicle" falls downward, it freezes the seawater it touches, forming a growing tube of ice. Anything the brinicle touches—such as sea stars caught in the wrong place at the wrong time—is killed instantly. That gives brinicles their nickname: the "icicles of death."

FROST FLOWERS

The last place you would expect to find blooming flowers is in the Arctic Ocean in the middle of winter. But that's exactly what you'd see—well, almost: These aren't actually garden flowers; they're delicate ice structures. Frost flowers develop when cold air above sea ice becomes saturated with water. Frost forms on tiny imperfections in the sea ice; as it collects more and more frost, an icy garden begins to grow.

GHOST APPLES

During a cold snap in 2019, a man was pruning trees in a western Michigan, U.S.A., orchard when he noticed these fantastic formations. The freezing rain and cold had turned the unpicked apples to mush, leaving behind an icy, "ghostly" shell after what was left of the apples slipped out the bottom.

GREEN FLASH

Beachgoers flock to the shore at sunset, hoping to catch sight of a strange ocean phenomenon called the green flash. It happens when the sun is almost below the horizon, with just its upper edge visible. For a second or two just before it dips out of sight, it can appear green in color. The green flash happens because of the way light is refracted through the atmosphere during a sunset. Water vapor absorbs the yellow and orange colors in white sunlight, and air molecules scatter the violet light, leaving just red and green light to travel to your eyes.

239

SPINNING FLAMES:
FIRE TORNADOES

There are few natural events more frightening than a wildfire. Walls of flames can tear through huge expanses of land, consuming hundreds of thousands of acres and leaving wastelands in their wake. But even scarier is a rare phenomenon that can take place inside a wildfire: a fire tornado.

Also known as a fire vortex or fire whirl, fire tornadoes aren't really tornadoes: They have more in common with whirlwinds or dust devils (p. 73), which typically form on hot sunny days when the ground heats the air above. Scientists are still learning about how fire tornadoes form. But they know that the intense heat caused by wildfires makes air rise. As new air rushes in to take its place, it can start to rotate. As the rotating column of air gets squeezed smaller by the air pushing in, it can speed up—similar to an ice skater pulling in his arms as he spins.

Most of the time, fire tornadoes are weak, short-lived, and occur in remote areas where people don't live. But on July 26, 2018, during the Carr Fire in California, a fire tornado that broke all the rules whirled into being. It had speeds of up to 165 miles an hour (266 km/h) and spun for an hour and a half. (A typical fire tornado lasts only a few minutes.) It went right through Redding, a city of 90,000 in the northern part of the state, near several national forests. It destroyed homes, trees, and transmission towers, as well as taking several lives and harming untold animals.

Fire tornadoes can be incredibly dangerous. As they form, they pick up burning embers, ash, debris, and flaming-hot gases and propel them as high as hundreds of feet into the air—potentially spreading the fire to surrounding areas. Experts are hard at work studying the many photographs and videos that were taken of the Carr Fire tornado and others, hoping to uncover how to predict and help prevent these deadly disasters in the future.

INTO THE FLAMES

When wildfires like the Carr Fire burn up in remote, hard-to reach areas, who goes to battle the blaze? That's a job for smokejumpers, elite firefighters who perform one of the most hazardous roles around—jumping out of planes right into the danger zone. After parachuting into the forest adjacent to the flames, they collect and carry more than 100 pounds (45 kg) of airdropped gear—everything they'll need to survive totally alone in the maelstrom for up to 48 hours. It takes mental toughness, extreme physical fitness, and intense training, but the brave men and women who accept the challenge can stave off disaster by stopping forest fires from turning into catastrophes.

The temperatures inside a fire tornado can reach more than 2000°F (1093°C).

EXTREME ELECTRICITY: LIGHTNING PHENOMENA

Ever since Benjamin Franklin bravely tied a key to a kite string and launched it skyward into a thunderstorm in the mid-18th century, we've known that lightning is a bolt of electricity flashing through the sky. Since then, we've discovered that there are all kinds of bizarre lightning strikes aside from the zigzag bolts we normally see. Here are a few of the strangest.

SPIDER LIGHTNING

Not all lightning strikes reach the ground. About three-quarters of all lightning never even leaves the cloud where it was formed. Instead, it seeks out a region of particles with the opposite charge within the thunderstorm. Sometimes these bolts are visible from the ground. They've earned the nickname "spider lightning" because they appear to creep and crawl along the underside of a cloud.

BALL LIGHTNING

What would you think if you saw a ball of light hovering above the ground, able to float through walls as if they weren't there? It seems too strange to be true, but people have been spotting exactly that since the time of the ancient Greeks. Experts were skeptical until 1963, when a scientist aboard a late-night flight saw a glowing orb fly down the airplane aisle and disappear though the wall just after lightning struck the plane. In the past few decades, ball lightning has been spotted in nature about 10,000 times, and scientists have even managed to re-create it in the lab, but they're still not sure what causes it to form.

VOLCANIC LIGHTNING

When molten rock pushes its way up through Earth's crust, it can break through the surface in a volcanic eruption. As if that's not dramatic enough, the ash plumes of some volcanoes contain lightning storms! Called volcanic lightning or a "dirty thunderstorm," these crackling displays occur because ash particles collide inside the plume, causing them to build up electrical energy that's released in a *zap!*

CATATUMBO LIGHTNING

The most electric place on Earth is where Venezuela's Lake Maracaibo meets the Catatumbo River. Here, there are about 260 stormy days per year, and a constant barrage of lightning strikes often illuminates the sky for the entire night. At the peak of storm season, around October, you can see an average of 28 flashes a minute! Scientists are still working to understand what exactly makes the area so high voltage.

DARK LIGHTNING

Lightning is one of nature's flashiest events. But recently, experts have discovered that it can also be invisible! Along with bright lightning bolts, thunderstorms release bursts of x-rays and even gamma rays, a form of radiation also emitted by collapsing stars far out in space. These invisible blasts, called dark lightning, can carry a million times as much energy as visible lightning, which shoots out in all directions instead of staying contained in one bolt.

A moonbow stretches across the landscape of Skjomen, near Narvik, Norway.

RAINBOWS AT NIGHT: MOONBOWS

Everybody knows about rainbows, the magical effect created by light from the sun passing through rain droplets (p. 44). Far more mysterious are moonbows, pale rainbows that can, under very special circumstances, appear on bright moonlit nights.

Moonbows form the same way as rainbows, except they are created by moonlight (sunlight reflected from the moon's surface) instead of sunlight. Because moonlight is much fainter than sunlight, moonbows are much dimmer than their rainbow cousins. And since our eyes don't see colors well in the dark, moonbows look like faint, white arches.

To spot a moonbow, you need to have clear skies and very bright moonlight, when the moon is almost full. Just like rainbows, moonbows can appear only if there are plenty of water droplets in the air. They've been spotted at the base of Yosemite Falls, when the spring snow melt has increased the amount of water running over the falls. They've also been seen in the cloud forests of Costa Rica, when winds blow in clouds of mist from late December to early February. And they've also occurred in random locations around the globe during nighttime rain showers around the time of the full moon.

But if you want the best chance of spotting a moonbow, there are only two places in the world you'd want to travel: Victoria Falls, on the border of Zambia and Zimbabwe; and Cumberland Falls, near Corbin, Kentucky, U.S.A. Whereas most waterfalls in the world are in deep ravines and gorges, both these falls are in wide gorges, allowing the moon's light to shine down on the mist kicked up by roaring water. If the sky is perfectly clear at just the right moment, a bright moonbow will appear suspended in the air over the falling water. It's one of nature's most stunning sights!

Bet You Didn't Know!

Double rainbows (and even double moonbows!) form when refracted light doesn't bounce out of the raindrop after being reflected the first time. Instead, the light reflects off of the inside of the raindrop a second time, producing a second, fainter rainbow above the first, with its colors reversed.

245

WHAT'S UP THERE?
RARE CLOUDS

Sometimes they look like fluffy animals floating across the sky; other times they are the dark and ominous warnings that a violent storm is on the way. But the clouds on these pages are another thing altogether: They're some of the world's weirdest and rarest cloud phenomena.

NACREOUS CLOUDS

You'd be lucky to spot nacreous clouds—they're some of the rarest on the planet. They form close to the poles during the coldest part of winter, when temperatures drop to below -117°F (-83°C). At that temperature, the atmosphere is very dry, so any small amounts of moisture condense into wispy clouds of ice crystals. Nacreous clouds form very high in the atmosphere, above 49,213 feet (15,000 m)— so high that the sun keeps illuminating them even after it has dropped below the horizon. That makes these clouds glow with spectacular colors against the dark sky.

KELVIN-HELMHOLTZ WAVE

Blink and you might miss it! Many cloud-spotters yearn to see this bizarre, short-lived formation. Looking just like cartoon waves, Kelvin-Helmholtz waves are caused when fast-moving warm air flows over a colder, slower-moving layer. When conditions are just right, perfect wavelike peaks appear at the boundary between the two layers. These clouds are highly unstable and will last for only a few minutes before disappearing.

FALLSTREAK HOLE

Have you ever seen a cloud that appears to have a piece missing from the middle? Then you've spotted a fallstreak hole, also called a hole punch cloud. This freaky effect is often caused by passing airplanes. When an aircraft zooms through a cloud of supercooled water droplets, it can cause air to expand and cool, making droplets freeze, form ice, and then fall. Other droplets cling to that falling ice and freeze, creating the distinctive hole shape.

MORNING GLORY CLOUDS

Between late August and October, hang gliders from around the world gather in the remote village of Burketown, Queensland, Australia, hoping to ride one of the world's rarest cloud phenomena: Morning Glory clouds. These narrow tubes, which are as long as 600 miles (966 km), form in sets of multiple clouds above where the Cape York Peninsula meets the Gulf of Carpentaria. When the winds from these two areas meet, they create a wave in the atmosphere that condenses into a visible cloud. Glider pilots can ride the updraft at the cloud's front edge for hundreds of miles.

LENTICULAR CLOUDS

These circular formations are often mistaken for alien spaceships. But they're just strangely shaped clouds. When moving, moist air comes across an obstacle—most often a mountain—the air is forced to head up and over it. As it rises, it cools and condenses into a cloud on the downwind side of the mountain. Because this cloud is continually being re-formed by moving air, the cloud appears to float in one place. Out of this world!

CHAPTER 13
SPACE WEATHER

Out in the vast emptiness of space, there's no weather at all. That's because with no atmosphere, there's no air moving around. But that doesn't mean conditions are comfortable: The International Space Station withstands extreme changes in temperature, from 250°F (121°C) in the light of Earth's sun to -250°F (-157°C) in the shade. And just like Earth, many planets—both in our solar system and those that spin around other suns—do have weather. If you think Earth's weather can be extreme, then get ready: These otherworldly worlds are rocked by winds that blow hundreds of miles a second and clouds that rain down rocks!

APOLLO 13

Outer space experiences extreme temperature shifts, and it also lacks oxygen and air pressure. When astronauts travel through space, they rely on their spacecraft to shelter them from this harsh environment. But what happens when that spacecraft fails?

On April 13, 1970, the crew of moon-bound Apollo 13 was about 200,000 miles (328,915 km) from Earth when something went wrong. The trio of astronauts heard the loud bang of an oxygen tank exploding, and warning lights in their instrument panel started flashing. "Houston, we've had a problem here," said pilot Jack Swigert. Commander Jim Lovell looked out the window and saw gas leaking out the rear of the spacecraft. It was oxygen. The astronauts were in big trouble.

Exposed wires in the oxygen tank had sparked, causing a fire that destroyed one oxygen tank and damaged the other. This was serious: The spacecraft's oxygen supply was critical to the crew's survival. It was mixed with hydrogen to make water and to generate power on their journey. And of course, they also needed it to breathe.

In an instant, flight controllers across the United States sprang into action. They quickly realized there was no way the crew could make it to the moon as planned. The new priority was getting the astronauts home safely on their damaged spacecraft. Luckily, the crew had a "lifeboat"—the lunar module, a craft meant to land them on the moon. It was still in perfect condition, but it was designed to take only two astronauts on a short trip from the moon's orbit to its surface—not carry a crew of three most of the way back to Earth. And although it was stocked with plenty of oxygen, it didn't have enough water, and it wasn't designed to filter enough air for three astronauts for several days.

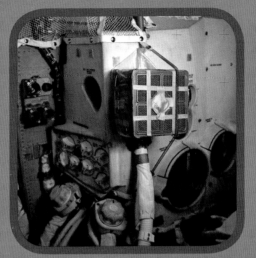

After putting the spacecraft on a trajectory back toward Earth, the crew powered down every non-essential system to lower the temperature and reduce the amount of water needed for cooling the machinery. Cabin temperatures dropped to about as 38°F (3.3°C). Moisture in the air condensed until all the walls and windows were dripping. The astronauts were soon shivering with cold—especially crew member Fred Haise, who had come down with a fever.

Meanwhile, engineers on the ground were working frantically to figure out how to keep all three astronauts alive in the lunar module. They came up with a plan that used a mishmash of supplies aboard Apollo 13, including the flight manual cover, duct tape, and a pair of socks, to reconfigure the module's air filters. It worked. The astronauts spent three days in the module, freezing cold and drinking only six ounces (177 mL) of water a day, which is one-fifth the normal intake. Mostly because of dehydration, the crew lost a total of 31.5 pounds (14 kg).

But throughout the four-day ordeal, the crew and flight controllers never lost their cool. As they neared Earth, they successfully powered up the main spacecraft and reentered Earth's atmosphere, splashing down in the South Pacific Ocean on April 17, 1970. Using smarts and skill, the astronauts had survived the harsh environment of space to become one of the greatest success stories in NASA history.

OPPOSITE: Jim Lovell, Jack Swigert, and Fred Haise head out for their mission.

TOP: The device to reconfigure the module's air filters was constructed by the crew from duct tape, maps, and other materials they had on hand.

ABOVE (FROM LEFT): Fred Haise, Jim Lovell, and Jack Swigert emerge from the recovery helicopter on board the aircraft carrier *Iwo Jima* on April 17, 1970.

STRANGE
SOLAR SYSTEM

Too hot to build a snowman? Too cold to go for a swim? The next time you're feeling like the weather just stole your thunder, you might want to check the forecast on Earth's neighbors. The extremes elsewhere in the solar system make Earth feel like cloud nine!

VENUS

Venus is often called Earth's "sister planet" because the two are so similar in size, composition, and orbit. But Venus is not a place you'd want to set up camp. At 900°F (465°C), its average temperature is hot enough to melt lead. As if that weren't unappealing enough, it's covered with clouds made of choking sulfuric acid and sulfur dioxide! And lightning storms, possibly caused by volcanic eruptions, regularly sizzle through its skies. Venus has very fast winds, and the atmospheric pressure at the surface is very high.

EARTH

THE SUN

You already know the sun is incredibly hot. After all, its light provides all of Earth's heat from a whopping 93 million miles (149.7 million km) away. But how hot is it? The sun's core burns at a temperature of about 27 million °F (15 million °C). That's pretty fiery! Solar storms also regularly rock the sun's surface, flinging showers of radiation and powerful magnetic fields outward toward the planets. Some even hit Earth!

MERCURY

With only a thin "exosphere," Mercury doesn't have weather events such as rain or wind. But it does have the most extreme fluctuations between hot and cold of any planet in the solar system. Because Mercury is the closest planet to the sun, it gets blasted by the sun's heat, reaching temperatures as high as 800°F (427°C). But when the sun sets, Mercury's surface drops to nearly -330°F (-201°C). Brrr!

MARS

At midday near the equator, the surface of Mars is a comfortable 70°F (20°C). But the red planet's thin atmosphere and distance from the sun means that near the poles in the winter, it can get as cold as -195°F (-125°C). The worst weather events on Mars, however, are regular dust storms kicked up in the rusty red dust that covers the planet's surface. They can blanket the entire planet and last for months!

SATURN

Things are pretty chill on Saturn ... literally! The average temperature here is a brisk -288°F (-178°C). Some winds here sweep the surface at 500 miles per second (1,800 km/s)—more than 7,000 times faster than the fastest-ever recorded wind speed on Earth—causing storms, hurricanes, and jet streams. On Earth, the heat energy that drives hurricanes comes from the sun's heat that is stored in the oceans; scientists believe that on Saturn, however, the heat that powers its hurricanes is generated deep inside the planet's interior.

URANUS

This far out in the solar system, temperatures drop way, *waaay* down—as cold as -371°F (-224°C)! Like the other gas giants (Saturn, Jupiter, and Neptune), Uranus features high winds and strong storms. But extreme weather reaches a whole new level on the seventh planet from the sun: Experts believe that in the immense pressure of the gas planet's interior, it may rain solid diamonds!

JUPITER

Jupiter has the most extreme weather of all the planets—so extreme it can be seen from Earth! Storms there can form within hours and grow to thousands of miles in size overnight. Wind speeds in these storms can reach 385 miles an hour (620 km/h)—well more than twice as fast as a Category 5 hurricane. One storm, the Great Red Spot, has been going since at least the late 1600s, when it was first observed by astronomers. The storm changes in size and has been measured at up to 24,855 miles (40,000 km) across—larger in diameter than Earth!

NEPTUNE

Like Uranus, Neptune may have diamond showers in its interior. But that's not all the wild weather there is on the farthest planet from the sun: It also has bands of storms that circle the planet, with wind speeds that have been clocked at an incredible 1,305 miles an hour (2,100 km/h). And during a 1989 flyby, NASA's Voyager 2 spacecraft spotted a raging cyclonic storm that measured 8,078 miles by 4,101 miles (13,000 by 6,600 km) across.

LOONY LUNAR EFFECTS: FAR-OUT MOONS

You might have heard the terms "blood moon," "blue moon," or "supermoon" before. But what do they mean? Can the moon actually change color? And what's so super about a supermoon?

Blood Moon

Sometimes, people say that the appearance of a "blood moon" is a prophecy of future events—but it's just an effect caused by Earth's atmosphere. "Blood moon" refers to the color of the moon during a total lunar eclipse. When this happens, the moon passes through the shadow of Earth cast by the sun. When the moon is completely blocked by Earth's shadow, it doesn't go completely dark: Instead, it turns deep red or reddish brown because some of the sunlight passing through Earth's atmosphere bends around the planet and falls on the moon's surface. Because that light is going through a thicker region of Earth's atmosphere, more of its blue light is scattered away, making the red and orange light more visible. It's the same effect that causes the brilliant colors of a sunset here on Earth.

Supermoon

Some believe supermoons can cause volcanic eruptions, earthquakes, and all kinds of terrible weather. In reality, though, there's nothing very strange or ominous about a supermoon at all. It happens because the moon's orbit isn't perfectly circular; it's elliptical, or shaped like an oval, meaning that the moon's distance from Earth is constantly changing. When the moon is full and also at its closest point to Earth, we call it a super-moon. But a supermoon is only about 6 percent closer than the average moon—a difference too small to be noticed by the human eye. And there's no connection between how the moon appears and weather events. Instead, if you've ever stepped outside at night to see a huge moon on the horizon looming above the treetops, it's likely that what you're actually seeing is the moon illusion—an optical illusion that makes the moon look bigger in the sky when it's near objects on Earth such as trees and buildings. Not so super after all!

Blue Moon

Despite the name, a blue moon doesn't have to do with color: It's just a nickname for the second full moon within a single calendar month. Since there are roughly 29.5 days between full moons, it's unusual for there to be two of them in a 30-day or 31-day month. The phenomenon happens only once every few years—the origin of the phrase "once in a blue moon." A blue moon may not be blue, but the moon can take on a blue hue in very rare circumstances, such as when particles of just the right size scatter red light, allowing blue light to pass through.

Bet You
Didn't
Know!

After the Indonesian volcano Krakatoa erupted in 1883, people in the area saw a blue-colored moon almost every night because of ash in the air.

A supermoon rises over a hillside in San Benito County, California.

WACKY MOON WEATHER

Like outer space, Earth's moon has no atmosphere and so, no weather. But it does have ice, which experts think may have been delivered by comet strikes. That ice stays frozen in the moon's deep craters, where sunlight never reaches. Astronomers who have measured the temperature inside—which reaches as low as -400°F (-240°C)—think these moon craters may be the coldest place in the entire solar system. But when it comes to crazy conditions, Earth's moon has nothing on these.

Bet You Didn't Know!

Saturn's moon Mimas has a huge crater that makes it look just like the Death Star space station from *Star Wars*.

TITAN

At first glance, Saturn's moon Titan is very much like Earth: It has a dense atmosphere, lakes on its surface, and clouds in its sky. But get closer and you'd find that they're not so similar after all. Those clouds and lakes aren't made of water; they're made of methane. Instead of a water cycle (p. 40), Titan has a methane cycle, driving seasonal rains of liquid methane that follow patterns similar to Earth's tropical monsoons (p. 76). The rains fill huge lakes, which slowly evaporate and condense into clouds, starting the cycle again.

ENCELADUS

If you like to ski, Enceladus might be your ideal vacation spot. The sixth-largest moon of Saturn has geysers that eject superfine ice particles, which fall back on the surface. The process is much slower than a snowstorm on Earth, but experts think that over tens of millions of years, it's likely that areas of Enceladus have become covered in powdery particles. Maybe future astronauts will hit the slopes!

IO

Jupiter's fifth moon would be a terrifying place to visit. It's the most volcanically active place in the solar system: Jupiter's gravity pulls so hard on Io that the moon is stretched and squeezed as it orbits, making its surface bulge up and down by as much as 328 feet (100 m). That causes molten sulfur beneath the surface to heat to the boiling point, then spew out of the hundreds of volcanoes that cover Io's surface. Some spew plumes of sulfur as high as 190 miles (300 km)! In the cold of space, the sulfur dioxide crystallizes into flakes, which fall back on the moon as fluffy, yellow sulfur snow.

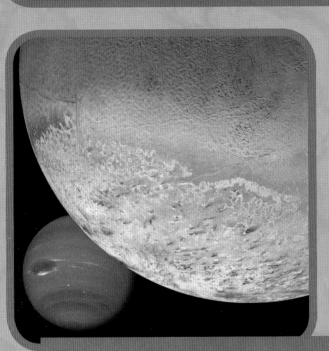

TRITON

The largest of Neptune's moons, Triton is extremely far from the sun: about 2.8 billion miles (4.5 billion km). But the sun's presence can still be felt on the frigid surface of Triton, which averages -391°F (-235°C). Scientists recently discovered that the icy moon has seasons just like Earth—but instead of a few months, they last 40 Earth years. As summer approaches, Triton's southern hemisphere warms up, causing frozen nitrogen, methane, and carbon monoxide on its surface to turn into gas and thicken the atmosphere.

Scientists think that there may be more water in rocks in the interior of Earth's moon than there is in all the U.S. Great Lakes combined.

257

WILD WORLDS: EXOPLANETS

History was made on January 9, 1992, when astronomers confirmed that there are planets outside of our solar system. Called exoplanets, they orbit their own suns, sometimes alone and other times as part of other solar systems. In the few short decades since that first discovery, scientists have identified thousands of these exoplanets. And they've discovered that some have weather almost stranger than science fiction.

It's Raining Rocks

Like Earth, planet CoRoT-7b is made mostly of rock. It also has a huge ocean similar to those found on our planet. But that's where the similarities end. CoRoT-7b is much, much closer to its sun than Earth is—about 60 times closer. That makes the planet unbearably hot at about 3990°F (2199°C).

It's so hot there, in fact, that the rock that makes up the planet's surface melts into liquid. A giant, reddish orange ocean of lava covers nearly half the planet. And that's not even the strangest thing about

Astronomers think the lava ocean on this planet is 28 miles (45 km) deep.

The pressure on Planet Gliese 1214b is extreme. It's equivalent to holding the weight of the *Titanic* on your pinky finger!

this place. Here, clouds made of vaporized rock float above the surface. When a weather front rolls in, that air condenses. But instead of raindrops, it forms pebbles that shower down on the surface of CoRoT-7b!

Steamy Skies

Planet Gliese 1214b is just 2.7 times bigger than Earth, but it weighs seven times as much. Scientists think it's heavy because it's a giant ball of water! At 450°F (232°C), the temperature of a hot oven, that heat instantly turns the water into steam here.

Here, the planet's strange sun—a red dwarf—paints the sky a glowing, soft pink. When the rosy sun sets, billions of tiny steam droplets in the atmosphere reflect its light. The pink sunlight and hazy sky create a colorful alien sunset unlike anything on Earth. Forecasters would have an easy job here: The weather is always cloudy! High above the planet's steamy surface float thick clouds. Experts think they could be made of potassium chloride—a type of salt.

Super Storms

On Earth, residents of Loma, Montana, U.S.A., experienced Earth's most extreme temperature swing ever recorded on January 15, 1972, when the temperature rose from -54°F (-48°C) to 49°F (9°C). That's 103 degrees (57°C) in 24 hours! But even that isn't anything like the weather on planet HD 80606b.

This planet has one wild orbit. It spends most of its time out away from its star, nearly as far as Earth is from our sun. But then, it hurtles in to within three million miles (4.8 million km) of its star (by contrast, Earth is 93 million miles (150 million km) from its star). Over the course of just six hours, the planet's temperature rises from 980 to 2240°F (528–1227°C)!

This rapid increase creates a huge buildup of energy. And that energy has to go somewhere: It causes an enormous storm—as wide as three Earths—that explodes out of the planet's surface. Twin hurricanes with long, spinning arms are born from the storm. They rip across the surface and head to the north and south poles, leaving behind a river of glowing gas that encircles the planet.

A violent storm rocks planet HD 80606b every 111 days—each time it passes its star.

A year on CoRoT-2b lasts only 1.7 days.

Melting Planet

From the surface of planet CoRoT-2b, this planet's sun dominates the sky. It's 1,000 times larger than the sun appears from Earth, and it's blotchy in appearance, dotted with dark sunspots. It's also spewing x-rays: the same form of energy a doctor uses to take pictures of broken bones.

Earth's sun emits x-rays, too, but on CoRoT-2b, they're a big problem. The sun is so close there that its gravity holds this planet in a death grip. All the while, it pummels the planet with x-rays a hundred thousand times more intense than Earth gets from our sun—radiation so extreme that it's literally evaporating the planet! Every second, it strips off about 4.5 million tons (4.1 million t) of matter from the planet's surface—the weight of 12 Empire State Buildings each time. The fierce radiation creates intense wind that blows the matter off the planet and into space.

GLOSSARY

ADAPTATION: a change to a living thing that makes it better fit its environment

ADVECTION: a horizontal movement of air that transfers a property of the atmosphere, such as heat or cold

AEROSOL: a tiny particle mixed into air or another gas

ALBEDO EFFECT: a measure of how much of the sun's energy is reflected back into space

ANTICYCLONE: a system of winds that rotate around a center of high atmospheric pressure, moving clockwise in the Northern Hemisphere and counterclockwise in the Southern Hemisphere

AQUIFER: an underground layer of rock with tiny holes that water can pass through

ATMOSPHERE: the layer of gases that surrounds Earth; also called air

ATMOSPHERIC PRESSURE: pressure exerted by the weight of air

BLIZZARD: a powerful snowstorm with low temperatures, strong winds, and large amounts of snow

BRUMATION: a condition of inactivity that some reptiles enter during winter

CARBON FOOTPRINT: the amount of carbon dioxide released into the atmosphere because of your own energy use

CLIMATE: the weather conditions in an area over a long period of time

CLIMATE CHANGE: a large difference in normal climate patterns over a long period of time

CLOUD: a collection of water droplets or ice crystals that forms in the sky

COLD-BLOODED: having a body temperature that changes with the environment; also called ectothermic

CONDENSATION: the process in which a gas changes to a liquid; the opposite of evaporation

CONDUCTOR: a material that transmits light, heat, sound, or electricity

CONTINENT: one of Earth's seven major areas of land

CONTINENTAL: relating to a continent

CORIOLIS FORCE: a force resulting from Earth's rotation that shifts moving objects to the right in the Northern Hemisphere and to the left in the Southern Hemisphere

CRUDE OIL: a form of fossil fuel formed from the buried remains of plants and animals that lived millions of years ago

CYCLONE: a powerful rotating storm that forms over warm oceans, specifically the Indian Ocean, the Bay of Bengal, and Australia (see also hurricane, typhoon)

DATA: information

DERECHO: a widespread, long-lasting windstorm associated with a fast-moving band of severe thunderstorms

DESERT: any large region that gets very little rain each year

DESERTIFICATION: the process of becoming desert

DEW POINT: the temperature at which a vapor, such as water, condenses (turns from a gas to a liquid)

DIURNAL: active during the day

DORMANT: a condition in which normal physical functions of a living thing shut down for a time

DOWNDRAFT: a downward current of air

DROUGHT: a period of below-average rainfall in a given area

EROSION: the process by which the surface of Earth is worn away by water, wind, waves, etc.

EVAPORATION: the process in which a liquid changes to a gas; the opposite of condensation

EXOPLANET: a planet outside our own solar system

FATA MORGANA: a complex type of mirage in which distant objects appear extremely distorted

FLOOD: a rising and overflowing of a large amount of water onto normally dry land

FOSSIL FUEL: a natural type of fuel such as coal, gas, or crude oil, formed in Earth from the remains of ancient plants and animals

FREEZING RAIN: rain that freezes when it hits a road or other solid object; also called glaze

FROSTBITE: freezing of the skin and body tissues caused by extreme cold

FUJITA SCALE: a scale for measuring the intensity of a tornado

GENERATOR: a machine that converts one form of energy into another

GLACIER: a slow-moving mass of ice

GLAZE: rain that freezes when it hits a road or other solid object; also called freezing rain

GREENHOUSE EFFECT: the trapping of the sun's heat in the planet's atmosphere

HABOOB: a violent dust storm or sandstorm

HAIL: a type of precipitation in the form of pellets of frozen rain

HEAT WAVE: a prolonged period of unusually hot weather

HEMISPHERE: half of Earth, such as dividing Earth by the Equator into the Northern Hemisphere and Southern Hemisphere

HIBERNATION: a condition of inactivity that some animals enter during winter

HURRICANE: a powerful rotating storm that forms over warm oceans, specifically the Atlantic Ocean, Gulf of Mexico, and the eastern Pacific Ocean (see also typhoon, cyclone)

HYPOXIA: a dangerous condition that happens when the body doesn't receive enough oxygen

ICE AGE: an extended period lasting millions of years in which thick ice sheets cover vast areas of land

ICE CORE: a long cylinder-shaped sample of ice removed from an ice sheet or glacier by drilling

ICE STORM: a storm of freezing rain that leaves a coating of ice

INFERIOR MIRAGE: a mirage in which an image of a distant object appears below the real object

INFRASOUND: sound of a frequency too low for human ears to hear

INSULATOR: a material that keeps energy, such as heat, from passing through

INTERGLACIAL: a period of warmer climate lasting thousands of years

JET STREAM: a narrow band of very strong air currents in the atmosphere

KATABATIC WIND: a wind that blows down a slope

LAND BREEZE: a breeze blowing toward the sea from land

LIGHTNING: a flash of light produced by a discharge of energy in the atmosphere

MARITIME: relating to the ocean

MESOVORTEX: a small, vertical whirl of air associated with a thunderstorm

METABOLISM: the chemical reactions within a body's cells that convert fuel from food into energy

METEOROLOGY: the science of the atmosphere, weather, and weather forecasting

MIGRATION: the periodic movement of groups of animals from one region to another

MODEL: a computer program that simulates different situations to make predictions

MOLECULE: the smallest unit of a substance that still has the properties of that substance

MONSOON: a seasonal wind pattern that causes rains and reverses direction between winter and summer

MOON ILLUSION: an optical illusion that causes the moon to appear larger when it is near the horizon

MULTICELL: a common thunderstorm consisting of multiple storm cells, or powerful updrafts and downdrafts moving in loops

NOCTURNAL: active at night

PERMAFROST: a permanently frozen layer of soil

PHOTOSYNTHESIS: the process by which green plants and some other organisms use sunlight to make their own food

PIGMENT: a colored material

POLAR ZONE: the part of Earth's surface located near the poles, characterized by a cold climate

POLAR EASTERLIES: winds that blow close to the North and South Poles, moving away from the poles and curving from east to west

PRECIPITATION: liquid and solid particles of water that fall from clouds, including rain, snow, and hail

RAIN: a type of precipitation in the form of liquid water droplets that fall to Earth

RADIOSONDE: a small measuring tool carried by balloon that measures information on atmospheric pressure, temperature, and humidity

REFRACTION: the bending of light as it passes from one substance to another

RENEWABLE RESOURCES: something found in nature and used by people that is naturally replaced, such as oxygen, fresh water, and solar energy

SEA BREEZE: a breeze blowing toward land from the sea

SILT: fine particles of soil carried along by flowing water

SNOW: a type of precipitation in the form of tiny crystals of ice that fall to Earth

SPECIALIST STORM CELL: an air mass formed by updrafts and downdrafts moving in loops; the smallest unit of a storm system

SUCCULENT: a plant adapted to dry conditions that has fleshy tissues for storing water

SUPERCELL: a type of thunderstorm containing a strong rotating updraft; has the potential to produce severe weather such as intense winds, large hail, and sometimes tornadoes

SUPERIOR MIRAGE: a mirage in which an image of a distant object appears above the real object

TEMPERATE ZONE: the part of Earth's surface between the Arctic Circle and the Tropic of Cancer and between the Antarctic Circle and the Tropic of Capricorn, characterized by a mild climate

THUNDERSTORM: a storm that produces lightning and thunder

TOPOGRAPHY: the physical features of an area such as mountains, rivers, lakes, and valleys

TORNADO: a violent rotating column of air that reaches from a thunderstorm down to the ground

TORPOR: a state of inactivity lighter than hibernation that some animals enter

TRADE WINDS: winds that occur near the equator and move from either the north or south toward the equator

TROPICAL ZONE: the part of Earth's surface located between the Tropic of Cancer and the Tropic of Capricorn; characterized by a hot climate

TUNDRA: a cold, treeless plain that covers about 20 percent of Earth's land surface

TYPHOON: a powerful rotating storm that forms over warm oceans, specifically the western Pacific Ocean (see also typhoon, cyclone)

UPDRAFT: an upward movement of air

WATER CYCLE: the constant movement of Earth's water. It evaporates from lakes, rivers, and oceans, forming water vapor, which rises, forms clouds, and falls as rain, hail, or snow.

WATER VAPOR: water that is in the form of a gas

WATERSPOUT: a whirling column of air and water mist

WAVELENGTHS: the distance between two points on a wave of sound or light

WEATHER BALLOON: a special type of balloon that carries instruments into the sky to measure weather data

WEATHER SATELLITE: an instrument that orbits Earth and monitors its weather and climate

WESTERLIES: winds that move from west to east in the mid-latitudes of the Northern and Southern Hemispheres

WILDFIRE: an uncontrolled fire burning in a forest, countryside, or other wilderness

WINDSTORM: a storm with winds strong enough to cause damage to trees and buildings

XEROCOLE: an animal adapted to live in the desert

FIND OUT
MORE

WEBSITES

Please ask permission from a parent or trusted adult before going online.

Get up-to-the-minute United States weather data from the National Oceanic and Atmospheric Administration (NOAA) Weather Service:
weather.gov

Find local forecasts and news at the Weather Channel website:
weather.com

Watch weather happening around the world at AccuWeather:
accuweather.com/en/world/satellite

Cover weather basics on the interactive DK Find Out! Weather website:
dkfindout.com/us/earth/weather/

Try out your weather-predicting skills and see what it's like to be a meteorologist at the Smithsonian Weather Lab:
ssec.si.edu/weather-lab

Play games and learn the answers to your questions at SciJinks, NASA and NOAA's weather website for kids:
scijinks.gov

Take your weather knowledge to the next level with JetStream, the National Weather Service's online school:
www.weather.gov/jetstream/

Learn about floods, tornadoes, hail, and more at the National Severe Storms Laboratory weather website:
nssl.noaa.gov/education/svrwx101/

Join Owlie and friends to play a game at the National Weather Service's Young Meteorologist program:
youngmeteorologist.org

Learn about magnetic storms, solar winds and more at the Space Science Institute's Space Weather Center:
spaceweathercenter.org/index.html

Check out meteorologist Crystal Wicker's weather website for kids:
weatherwizkids.com

Plan ahead for natural disasters at ready.gov, the U.S. Department of Homeland Security's weather preparedness planning website:
ready.gov

MOVIES & TV

• *Destructive Weather* (2017): When does weather turn dangerous? Find out in this BBC documentary.

• *Extreme Weather* (2016): This National Geographic documentary explores how climate change is influencing weather around the world.

• *Storm Chasers* (2007): Follow storm chasers as they fearlessly hunt down tornadoes in this Discovery Channel series.

• *When Weather Changed History* (2008): From the space shuttle *Challenger* explosion to the American Dust Bowl, learn how weather has shaped all kinds of events in this series from the Weather Channel.

• *Wild Weather* (2017): Take a deeper look at the forces that create weather in this PBS show.

• *The World's Worst Disasters* (2009): This Netflix series details history's most destructive floods, cyclones, hurricanes, and more.

PLACES TO VISIT

• Museum of Science and Industry, Chicago Weather Wise Learning Lab:
www.msichicago.org/education/field-trips/learning-labs/weather-wise/

• National Weather Museum and Science Center in Norman, Oklahoma:
nationalweathermuseum.com

BOOKS

• *DK Eyewitness Books: Hurricane and Tornado* by Jack Challoner

• *DK Eyewitness Books: Weather* by Brian Cosgrove

• *DK Smithsonian Eyewitness Explorer Weather Watcher: Explore Nature With Loads of Fun Activities*

• *The Kids' Book of Weather Forecasting* by Mark Breen

• *National Geographic Extreme Weather Survival Guide: Understand, Prepare, Survive, Recover* by Thomas M. Kostigen

• *National Geographic Kids Everything Weather: Facts, Photos, and Fun That Will Blow You Away* by Kathy Furgang

• *National Geographic Kids Extreme Weather: Surviving Tornadoes, Sandstorms, Hailstorms, Blizzards, Hurricanes, and More!* by Thomas M. Kostigen

INDEX

Boldface indicates illustrations.

A

Adélie penguins **188,** 188–189, **189**
Advection fog 48, **49**
Aerosols 46
African bullfrogs 163, **163**
Agriculture
   and climate change 227
   sustainable farming 122, 231
Air: role in weather 16, 17, **17**
Air pressure 17, 26, 28, 31, 67, 85
Air quality 227
Airplanes
   and fallstreak holes 247
   grounded by heat waves 89, **89**
   hurricane hunters 30, **30**
   smokejumpers 240, **240**
   uplift 74–75, 89
   weather phenomena 45, 237, 242
Albedo effect 167
Alligators **212,** 212–213, **213**
Alps, Europe 107, **107,** 220
Altocumulus clouds 47, **47**
Altostratus clouds 47, **47**
Amazon rainforest, South America
   anacondas 135, **135**
   dust from Sahara 95
   indigenous people **122,** 122–123, **123**
   rainfall 117, 118, 123
   survival story 118–119
   threats to 229
Amazon River, South America 123, **123**
American alligators **212,** 212–213, **213**
Amundsen, Roald **168,** 168–169
Amundsen-Scott South Pole Station, Antarctica **169**
Andes, South America 196, 220
Animals
   and climate change 140, 178, 207, 211, 224–225
   of the desert 154–163, **154–163**
   nocturnal 137, 154, 206–207, **206–207**
   at the Poles 176–189, **176–189**
   in the temperate zone 202–215, **202–215**
   of the tropics 124–141, **125–141**
   and weather prediction 32–33
Antarctica
   climate 145, 167
   glaciers **104**
   ice-core research 113, **220**
   ice sheets 104, 105, 167, 220
   notothenioid fish 182, **182**
   penguins **164,** 177, **177, 188,** 188–189, **189**
   race to the South Pole **168,** 168–169, **169**
   research stations 104–105, **105, 169,** 174
   as uninhabited 174
   Weddell seals **186,** 186–187, **187**
Apollo 13 **250,** 250–251, **251**
Appalachian Trail, U.S.A. **194,** 194–195
Apple trees: ice formations 239, **239**
Aral Sea, Kazakhstan-Uzbekistan 92, **92**
Arctic foxes 177
Arctic Ocean
   currents 177
   frost flowers 239, **239**
   orcas 183
Arctic people 170–173, **171–173**
Arica, Chile 87, **87**
Ash, volcanic 220, 243, 255
Atacama Desert, Chile 87, 148
Auroras 14, **14**

B

Bactrian camels **144, 158,** 158–159, **159**
Ball lightning 242, **242**
Barometers 26
Beavers 231, **231**
Bedouin 151, **151**
Big Salt Marsh, Kansas, U.S.A. **93**
Bjerknes, Jacob and Vilhelm 27
Black-tailed jackrabbits 155, **155,** 211
Blacktip sharks 32
Blizzards 20, **108,** 108–109, 167, 223
Blood moons 254, **254**
Blowguns 122, **122**
Blue moons 255, **255**
Blue morpho butterflies **128,** 128–129, **129**
Blue sky 200–201, **201**
Bowhead whales 183, **183**
Brinicles 238, **238**
Brown bears **204,** 204–205
Brumation 202, 212
Bryce Canyon National Park, Utah, U.S.A. 53, **53**
Bubbles, frozen 108, **108,** 238, **238**
Buffalo, New York, U.S.A. 109, **109**
Burketown, Queensland, Australia 247

C

Cactuses 136, 154, **154,** 161
California
   drought 92
   wildfires 222, **222,** 240
Cambyses II, King (Persian Empire) 148
Camels **92, 144,** 150, **150, 158,** 158–159, **159**
Cape ground squirrels 163, **163**
Cape Town, South Africa 226
Carbon dioxide 17, 113, 117, 220, 230, 231
Caribou 170, 172, 173, **180,** 180–181, **181**
Carr Fire (2018) 240, **241**
Catatumbo lightning 243, **243**
Cave of Crystals, Chihuahua, Mexico 52, **52**
Cerro Blanco, Sechura Desert, Peru 79, **79**
Chlorophyll 198, 199
Cirrocumulus clouds 47, **47**
Cirrostratus clouds 47, **47**
Cirrus clouds 47, **47**
Climate change
   and animals 140, 178, 207, 211, 224–225
   battle against 230–231

desertification 145, 231
disappearing places **228,** 228–229, **229**
extreme weather 140, 222, 227
future predictions 83, 145, 221, 222–223, 228, 229
global warming 101, 167, 217–220, 227
ice ages and interglacials 220
impact on human life 226–227
melting ice 113, 170, 178, 220, 224
record high temperatures 86, 219
rising sea levels 219, 220, 221, 228, 229
role of fossil fuels 219, 230
and tropical rainforests 117, 229, 230–231
Climate vs. weather 20
Clouds
cloud-to-ground lightning **37,** 56
intracloud lightning 56
rare phenomena **246,** 246–247, **247**
thunderclouds 55, **55,** 56
types of 46–47, **47**
Cold fronts 29, **29**
Collared peccaries **136,** 136–137, **137**
Condensation 41, 42, 46, 48
Coral islands 229, **229**
Corals and coral reefs 53, 152, **152,** 225, **225**
Coriolis force 68, 69
Corn
"corn hail" 75, **75**
crop damage **84,** 222
CoRoT-2b (exoplanet) 261, **261**
CoRoT-7b (exoplanet) 258–259
Costa Rica
cloud forests 245
rainforest 140
renewable power 230
Cows 74, 127, 215
Crickets 9, **9**
Crocodiles 212, **212,** 220
Cryosphere 113, **113**
Cumberland Falls, Kentucky, U.S.A. 245
Cumulonimbus clouds 47, **47**

D

Dark lightning 243, **243**
Dawes Glacier, Alaska **221**
Death Valley, California, U.S.A. 86, **86**
Deforestation 117, 219, 229, 231
Derechos 55, **55**
Desert zones 142–163, **142–163**
Desertification 145, 231
Dew 9, 160, 162
Dew point 42, 48
Diseases 112, 123, 170, 227
Dogsleds 172, **172**
Doppler effect 31
Doppler radar 71
Double rainbows 245, **245**
Droughts **92,** 92–93, **93,** 222, 225–228
Dunhuang Yardang National Geopark, Gansu Province, China 79, **79**
Dust devils 73, **73,** 75, **75,** 240
Dust storms 80, **94,** 95, **95,** 148, **149,** 252

E

Earth (planet)
atmosphere **12,** 12–13, **13,** 17
magnetic field 14, 215
orbit 193
rotation 68
seasons **100,** 193, **193,** 198–199
tilt 167, 193, 199
water 42, **42**
wind patterns **68,** 68–69, **69**
see also Climate change
East Antarctic Ice Sheet 104, 105
Echidnas 202, **202**
Eggs: cooking on sidewalks **90,** 90–91, **91**
El Niño 99
Elephants 32, **112**
Ellicott City, Maryland, U.S.A. 59
Elves (flashes of light) 15, **15**
Emperor penguins **164,** 177, **177**
Enceladus (moon of Saturn) 257, **257**
European badgers 207, **207**
Evaporation 41, 85, 145, 148, 222, 223
Exoplanets 258–261, **258–261**
Exosphere 13, **13**

F

Fahrenheit, Daniel 26
Fall foliage **190–191,** 198, **198,** 199
Fallstreak holes 247, **247**
False tree coral snakes 134, **134**
Farming. see Agriculture
Fennec foxes **142–143, 156,** 156–157, **157**
Ferrar Glacier, Antarctica **104**
Fire tornadoes 240–241, **241**
Firefighters 240, **240**
Fires. see Forest fires; Wildfires
Floods **58,** 58–59, **76,** 223, **223,** 227
Fog 48, **48,** 49, **49,** 148, 161
Fog catchers 148, **148**
Fogstand beetles **160,** 161
Forest fires **82,** 83, **83, 216–217,** 220, 240
Fossil fuels 219, 230
Franklin, Benjamin 56, 242
Freezing fog 48, **48**
Frost flowers 239, **239**

G

Galveston, Texas, U.S.A.: hurricane (1900) 38–39, **38–39**
Gamma rays 243
Gatewood, Emma **194,** 194–195, **195**
Ghinsberg, Yossi **118,** 118–119, **119**
Glacier National Park, Montana, U.S.A. 228, **228**
Glaciers 83, **104,** 113, **113,** 219, 220, **221,** 228
Gliese 1214b (exoplanet) 259, **259**
Global warming 101, 167, 218, 219, 227
Gobi desert, Asia **144,** 145, 150, 158
Goblin Valley State Park, Utah, U.S.A. 78, **78**
Golden eagles 150, **150**
Golden poison frogs 122
Golden-winged warblers 32, 33, **33**
Grand Canyon, Arizona, U.S.A. 52, **52**
Graupel 42
Great Blue Hole, Belize 53, **53**
Greater roadrunners 163, **163**
Greeks, ancient 25, 44, 56, 152
Green, Benjamin 152
Green anacondas 135, **135**
Green flash 239, **239**

Greenhouse effect 219
Greenland
    caribou 181
    ice sheet 220, 221
    indigenous people 170
    Vikings 170
Ground squirrels 163, **163,** 205
Groundhogs 25, **25,** 202

H
Ha Long Bay, Vietnam 53, **53**
Haboobs **94,** 95, **95, 149**
Hail 8, **8,** 42, 50–51, **50–51,** 75, **75,** 95
Haise, Fred **250,** 250–251, **251**
HD 80606b (exoplanet) 260, **260**
Heat waves
    in ancient times 25
    and climate change 86, 222, 226, 227
    Europe (2003) **82,** 82–83, **83,** 85
    safety during 85
    strange effects of 88–89
    world record 87
Hibernation 198, 199, 202, 205, 207, 208, 225
Hoodoos 53, **53**
Hot air balloons 18, 201, **201**
Hurricane Charley (2004) 32
Hurricane Harvey (2017) 38, 40, 223
Hurricane hunters 30, **30**
Hurricane Irma (2017) 38, 39, 228
Hurricane Maria (2017) 38
Hurricane Sandy (2012) 61
Hurricane Wilma (2005) **60**
Hurricanes 30, 38–39, **38–39, 60,** 60–61, **61,** 223
Hypoxia 196

I
Ice
    ancient 112–113, **113**
    brinicles 238, **238**
    frost flowers 239, **239**
    hailstones 8, **8,** 50, **50–51,** 51, 95
    see also Sea ice
Ice ages 53, 220
Ice cores 113, **175,** 220
Ice fishing 173, **173**
Ice storms 101, 110, **110,** 110–111, **111**
Igloos 173, **173**
Industrial Revolution 219, 230

Interglacials 220
International Space Station (ISS) 30, **30,** 248
Inuit people 169, 170, 172, **172, 173**
Io (moon of Jupiter) 257, **257**
Iowa, U.S.A.: radar trucks **22–23, 34**

J
Jackrabbits 154, 155, **155,** 211
Jet streams 68, **68,** 85, 99, 253
Jupiter (planet) 14, 253, **253,** 257

K
Kangaroo rats 154, **154**
Kansas, U.S.A.: landspout tornado **21**
Katabatic winds 167
Kayapo people 121, **121**
Keas 138, **138**
Kelvin-Helmholtz waves 246, **246**
Key West, Florida, U.S.A. 66, **66,** 228, **228**
Khartoum, Sudan **149**
Kilchurn Castle, Scotland **49**
Kilimanjaro, Mount, Tanzania **112**
Kiwis 207, **207**
Koalas 207, **207**
Krakatoa (island volcano), Indonesia 255, **255**

L
Las Vegas, Nevada, U.S.A.: water 151
Lenticular clouds 247, **247**
Lightning
    bizarre kinds of 242–243, **242–243**
    chances of getting hit 57
    cloud-to-ground lightning **37,** 56
    how it is created 55, 56, 237
    intracloud lightning 56
    myths and legends 25, 56
    speed and temperatures 8, 56
    volcanic lightning **233,** 243, **243**
Lima, Peru: fog catchers 148, **148**
Little brown bats 206, **206**
Loma, Montana, U.S.A. 260
Los Angeles, California: rainfall 92
Lovell, Jim **250,** 250–251, **251**

M
Macaws **138,** 138–139, **139**
Magnetic fields 14, 215, 252
Malaria 123, 227
The Maldives, Indian Ocean 229, **229**
Mangrove forests 61, **61**
Marathon des Sables (race) 146, 147
Marble Bar, Australia: heat wave (1923–24) 87
Marmots 225, **225**
Mars (planet) 73, 79, 252, **252**
Mercury (planet) 201, 252, **252**
Mesopotamia 196
Mesosphere 13, **13**
Meteorites 15, **15**
Meteorology
    aerial weather observation 30–31, **30–31**
    history 25
    measuring tools 26–27, **26–27,** 28
    time line 26–27
    weather forecasting 28–29, **29,** 30, 31
Meteors 12, 13
Mexico
    crystal cave 52, **52**
    desert life 154, 155
    drought (2011) 227
    monarch butterflies 208
    monsoon 77
Mexico, Gulf of 33, 39, 71, 73, 77
Miami, Florida, U.S.A.: hurricane (2005) **60**
Mimas (moon of Saturn) 256, **256**
Mirages **234,** 234–235, **235**
Monarch butterflies 208, **208, 209**
Mongolia
    camels **144,** 158, **159**
    nomadic people 150, **150**
    weather 77, 101, 158
Monsoons **76,** 76–77, **77**
Moon
    blue moons 255, **255**
    craters 256
    eclipses 254, **254**
    ice 256
    orbit 251, 255
    supermoons 255, **255**
Moon missions. see Apollo 13

Moonbows **244,** 244–245
Moons, planetary 256–257, **256–257**
Morning glory clouds 247, **247**
Morse, Samuel 26
Mosquitoes 123, **123,** 206, 227
Mudslides 59, **59**
Mummies **106,** 106–107
Myths and legends 25, 44, 56

N
Nacreous clouds 246, **246**
Namib desert beetles **160,** 161
Narwhals 183, **183**
Needles, California, U.S.A. 87
Neptune (planet) 14, 253, **253, 257**
New Zealand
    keas 138, **138**
    kiwis 207, **207**
    wind-bent trees 78, **78**
Nimbostratus clouds 47, **47**
Nocturnal animals 137, 154, 206–207, **206–207**
Norse mythology 25, 44, 56
North American monsoon 77
North Atlantic Oscillation 99
North Pole 101, 167, 169, 170, 193
Northern Hemisphere 68, 69, 71, 193, 198, 199
Northwest Passage 168, 234
Notothenioid fish 182, **182**

O
Optical illusions 44, 234, 255
Orangutans 115, 124, **133,** 224, **224**
Orcas 176, **176,** 183, **183**
Orchid mantises 125, **125**
Ötzi the Iceman (mummy) **106,** 106–107
Oymyakon, Russia 105, **105**

P
Pacific Ocean
    climate patterns 99
    tropical cyclones 61
    underwater heat wave (2016) 88
Pangaea (supercontinent) 174
Paradise tree snakes 134, **134**
Parson's chameleons **130,** 130–131
Peccaries **136,** 136–137, **137**

Penguins **164,** 177, **188,** 188–189, **189**
Permafrost 113, **113**
Photosynthesis 154, 199
Polar bears **89, 166,** 177–179, **178, 179,** 224, **224**
Porcupines 206, **206**
Portugal: forest fires **82, 83**
Prisms 200, **200**
Prosperi, Mauro **146,** 146–147

Q
Quivira National Wildlife Refuge, Kansas, U.S.A. **93**

R
Radar 30, 31, 35, 71
Radar trucks **22–23, 34,** 35, 71, **71**
Radiation fog 48, **49**
Radiosondes 30, 31, **31**
Rain
    animals and **132,** 132–133, **133**
    in the spring 199, **199**
    water cycle 40–41, **40–41**
Rain fog 48, **48**
Rainbows 9, **9,** 25, **44,** 44–45, **45,** 245, **245**
Rainforests, temperate 194, 195
Rainforests, tropical
    and carbon dioxide 117, 230–231
    human inhabitants 120–123, **120–123**
    layers 124, **124**
    plants and animals 123, **123,** 124–141, **125–141**
    poor soils 95, 120
    weather patterns 20, 117
    see also Amazon rainforest
Red foxes **214,** 214–215, **215**
Regent, Sierra Leone 59
Roopkund (lake), India: skeletons 50, **50**
Ross, John 234
Ross Sea **220**

S
Saguaro cactuses 154, **154**
Sahara desert, Africa
    dust storms 94, 95
    fennec foxes 157
    search for "lost army" 148

survival story 146–147
temperatures 145
Sahel (region), Africa 231, **231**
San Francisco, California, U.S.A.:
    fog 49, **49**
San Francisco Bay, California, U.S.A.: sailboats **16**
Sandgrouse 162, **162**
Sandstorms 145, 147, 148, 151, 158
Satellites 13, **13,** 27, **27,** 39, 105
Saturn (planet) 14, 253, **253,** 257
Scarlet macaws **138,** 138–139, **139**
Scott, Robert Falcon **168,** 168–169
Sea ice
    brinicles 238, **238**
    frost flowers 239, **239**
    ice fishing 173, **173**
    Inupiat words for 110
    leads 183, **183**
    melting 167, 178, 224
    and polar bears 178, 224
    role in Earth's climate 167
Sea-level rise 53, 219, 220, 221, 228, 229
Sea turtles 225, **225**
Seasons **100,** 193, **193,** 198–199
Seattle, Washington, U.S.A.:
    rainfall 92
Sharks 32, 33, 53, 215
Shilin Stone Forest, Yunnan Province, China 79, **79**
Shooting stars 15, **15**
Silver Spring, Maryland, U.S.A. 99, **99**
Sinkholes 53, **53**
Slope Point, South Island, New Zealand 78, **78**
Sloths **126,** 126–127, **127,** 140
Smog 227, **227**
Smokejumpers 240, **240**
Snakes 134–135, **134–135**
Snowflakes 31, 42, **102,** 102–103
Snowshoe hares **210,** 210–211, **211**
Snowstorms **98,** 98–99, **99,** 223, **223**
Snowy owls **184,** 184–185, **185**
Solar system 252–253, **252–253**
Sonoran Desert, Mexico–U.S.:
    cactuses **154**
South Africa
    bushmen 148, **148**
    see also Cape Town

South Pole 78, 100, 101, 105, 167–169, **168, 169**
Southern Hemisphere 68, 69, 101, 104, 193
Southern right whales 202
Space weather 248–261, **248–261**
Spearfish, South Dakota, U.S.A. 87
Spider lightning 242, **242**
Spider monkeys **140**, 140–141, **141**
Sprites (flashes of light) 15, **15**
St. Elmo's fire **236**, 237, **237**
Storm chasers **23, 34**, 34–35, **72**, 74
Stratocumulus clouds 47, **47**
Stratosphere 13, **13**, 68
Stratus clouds 47, **47**
Summer solstice 198
Sun 10, 252, **252**
Sunlight
    colors 200, **200**
    and photosynthesis 154, 199
    role in weather 18, **18**
    sunniest place on Earth 9, **9**
Sunscreen 152
Sunsets 15, **15**, 239, **239**, 254
Supercells 35, **36–37**, 55, 73
Supermoons 255, **255**
Swallows 202, **203**
Swigert, Jack **250**, 250–251, **251**

T

Tanamachi, Robin **23, 34**, 34–35
Telegraphs 26, **26**
Temperate zone 192–215, **192–215**
Thermometers, mercury 26, **26**
Thermosphere 13, **13**
Thor (Norse god) **24**, 25, 56
Thorny devils 160, 162, **162**
Three-toed sloths **126**, 126–127, **127**
Thunder 25, 55, 56
Thunderclouds 55, **55**, 56
Thunderstorms **54**, 54–55, **55**
    supercells 35, **36–37**, 55, 73
    wind speeds 55, 71
Titan (moon of Saturn) 256, **256**
Tongass National Forest, Alaska, U.S.A.: glacier **221**
Tornadoes **21**, 64–65, **64–65**, 72–75, **72–75**
Torricelli, Evangelista 26, **26**
Trade winds 68, 69, **69**, 117

Tree rings 220
Tri-State Tornado (1925) 64–65, **64–65**
Triton (moon of Neptune) 257, **257**
Tropical cyclones 61, **70**, 71, 117
Tropical storms 32, 33, 60, 61, 110
Tropical zone 114–141, **114–141**
Troposphere 13, **13**, 73
Typhoons 61, 117

U

Ultraviolet (UV) light 128, 152, 181
Unionville, Maryland, U.S.A. 58
Uranus (planet) 14, 253, **253**

V

Valley fog 48, **48**
Veiled chameleons 131, **131**
Venice, Italy 229, **229**
Venus (planet) 252, **252**
Victoria Falls, Zambia-Zimbabwe 245
Volcanic ash 220, 243, 255
Volcanic eruptions 243, **243**, 252, 255, **255**
Volcanic lightning **233**, 243, **243**
Vostok Station, Antarctica 104–105, **105**

W

Walruses 178, 182, **182–183**
Warm fronts 29, **29**
Washington, D.C.
    full moon **255**
    snowstorm 98, **99**
Washington, Mount, New Hampshire, U.S.A. 71, **71**, 195
Water
    amount on Earth 42, **42**
    landforms shaped by **33, 52**, 52–53
    role in weather 18, **18**
    shortages 26, 154
    supply 83, 92, 226
    water cycle 40, **40–41**
Waterfalls **18–19**, 245
Waterspouts 9, **9**, 73, **73**
Wave Rock, Australia 53, **53**
Weather balloons 31, **31**
Weather forecasting 28–29, **29**, 30, 31

Weather maps 26, **27, 28–29**
Weather vs. climate 20
Weddell Sea **174**
Weddell seals **186**, 186–187, **187**
White-lipped island pit vipers 135, **135**
Wildfires 77, 86, 92, 202, 222, **222**, 240
Wind
    formation of 17, 67
    global patterns **68**, 68–69, **69**
    highest wind speed 71
    jet streams 68, **68**, 85, 99, 253
    landforms shaped by **78**, 78–79, **79**
Wind farms 67, **67**
Wind power 67, 230
Winter solstice 198
Wood frogs 205, **205**
Woolsey Fire (2018) 222, **222**
World War I 27
World War II 27, 65, 83, 152

X

X-rays 243, 261
Xerocoles 154
Xingu River, Brazil 121, **121**

Y

Yanomami people 120, **120**
Yardangs 79, **79**
Yuma, Arizona, U.S.A. 9, **9**

Z

Zeus (Greek god) 56
Zinder Valley, Niger 231

PHOTO & ILLUSTRATION CREDITS

COVER: (frog), Michael Durham/Minden Pictures; (lightning), Anna Omelchenko/Shutterstock; (snowboarder), Dennis van de Water/Shutterstock; (water droplet background), Mario7/Shutterstock; (hurricane), Harvepino/Shutterstock; (umbrella), heromen30/Shutterstock; (windsock), Kletr/Shutterstock; back cover (snowflake), Kichigin/Shutterstock; (boots), sl_photo/Shutterstock; (tornado), Minerva Studio/Shutterstock; spine (snowflake), Kichigin/Shutterstock; flap: (UP), Stephanie Warren Drimmer; (LO), Luigino De Grandis; (sunglasses), studiovin/Shutterstock

VARIOUS THROUGHOUT: (raindrop background), Mr Twister/Shutterstock; (clouds background), Bplanet/Shutterstock; (rippled sand background), Chaikovskiy Igor/Shutterstock; (cracked earth background), HeinSchlebusch/Shutterstock; (streaky cloud background), Sunny Forest/Shutterstock; (palm leaves background), Vibe Images/Shutterstock; (frost background), Olga Miltsova/Shutterstock

FRONT MATTER: 1, Mark Hamblin/Photographer's Choice/Getty Images; 2, RomanKhomlyak/iStockphoto/Getty Images; 4, James Braund/Taxi/Getty Images; 5 (UP), Jim Reed; 5 (LO LE), Chuck Franklin/Alamy Stock Photo; 5 (LO RT), Mike Hill/Alamy Stock Photo; 6, Nataliya Burnley; 7 (UP), Luigino De Grandis; 7 (LO), Kichigin/Shutterstock; 8 (UP), Photodisc; 8 (LO LE), Mike Theiss/National geographic Image Collection; 8 (LO RT), Ron Levi/EyeEm/Getty Images; 9 (UP LE), Cheri Alguire/iStockphoto/Getty Images; 9 (UP RT), encikAn/Shutterstock; 9 (LO), Toshi Sasaki/Photographer's Choice/Getty Images

CHAPTER 1: 10-11, Sarah Beard Buckley/Moment RM/Getty Images; 12, NASA; 13, Sanjida Rashid/NGK Staff; 14, John A Davis/Shutterstock; 15 (UP), David Aguilar; 15 (CTR), S.Borisov/Shutterstock; 15 (LO), Stephane Vetter; 16, Martin Sundberg/Uppercut RF/Getty Images; 17, Sanjida Rashid/NGK Staff; 18-19, Bamboosil/age fotostock; 18 (BOTH), Sanjida Rashid/NGK Staff; 20-21, Jim Reed

CHAPTER 2: 22-23, Ryan McGinnis/Alamy Stock Photo; 24, Fotokostic/Shutterstock; 25, Jeff Swensen/Getty Images; 26 (UP), INTERFOTO/Alamy Stock Photo; 26 (LO LE), Chronicle/Alamy Stock Photo; 26 (LO RT), Ian Poole/Dreamstime; 27 (UP LE), Pilvitus/Shutterstock; 27 (UP RT), Bettmann Creative/Getty Images; 27 (LO LE), Keystone-France/Gamma-Keystone/Hulton Archive Creative/Getty Images; 27 (LO RT), Science History Images/Alamy Stock Photo; 28-29, Pilvitus/Shutterstock; 29, Lawrence Migdale/Science Source; 30 (UP), NOAA; 30 (LO), NASA; 31 (BOTH), NASA; 33 (UP), Amilevin/Dreamstime; 33 (LO), Jayne Gulbrand/Shutterstock; 34 (UP), Ryan McGinnis/Alamy Stock Photo; 34 (LO), Robin L. Tanamachi

CHAPTER 3: 36-37, Jim Reed; 38-39, Leemage/UIG/Getty Images; 39, Library of Congress/Corbis/VCG/Getty Images; 40, Florin Stana/Shutterstock; 40-41, Merkushev Vasiliy/Shutterstock; 41 (UP), Mr Twister/Shutterstock; 41 (CTR), Sunny Forest/Shutterstock; 41 (LO), Willyam Bradberry/Shutterstock; 42, Howard Perlman, USGS/globe illustration by Jack Cook, Woods Hole Oceanographic Institution; 43, Bob Thomas/Photographer's Choice/Getty Images; 44 (LE), Stuart Armstrong; 44 (RT), mrjew/Shutterstock; 45 (UP), hphimagelibrary/Gallo Images/Getty Images; 45 (LO), Chakarin Wattanamongkol/Moment RF/Getty Images; 46, Gary Hincks/Science Source; 47 (UP-A), Joyce Photographics/Science Source; 47 (UP-B), Jim Reed; 47 (UP-C), C_Eng-Wong Photog/Shutterstock; 47 (CTR-A), Mark A. Schneider/Science Source; 47 (CTR-B), Dorling Kindersley ltd/Alamy Stock Photo; 47 (CTR-C), Jim Reed; 47

(LO-A), Koncz/Shutterstock; 47 (LO-B), David R. Frazier/Science Source; 47 (LO-C), Aaron Haupt/Science Source; 47 (LO-D), ZT Martinusso/Moment RF/Shutterstock; 48, imageBROKER/Alamy Stock Photo; 48 (CTR), Lowell Georgia/Science Source; 48 (LO), Andre Gilden/Alamy Stock Photo; 49, nagelestock.com/Alamy Stock Photo; 49 (INSET), Francesco Carucci/Shutterstock; 50-51, adamada/Shutterstock; 50, Awanish Tirkey/Shutterstock; 51 (UP), NWS Aberdeen/NOAA; 51 (CTR), JJS-Pepite/iStockphoto/Getty Images; 51 (LO), Michael Thompson; 52 (UP), Carsten Peter/Speleoresearch & Films/National Geographic Image Collection; 52 (LO), Amineah/Shutterstock; 53 (UP LE), Tami Freed/Shutterstock; 53 (UP RT), Pierre Leclerc/Shutterstock; 53 (LO LE), PhotoRoman/Shutterstock; 53 (LO RT), David Steele/Shutterstock; 54, MinervaStudio/Dreamstime; 55 (UP), Jim Reed/Science Source; 55 (LO), Claus Lunau/Science Source; 56, diez artwork/Shutterstock; 57, Mihai Simonia/Shutterstock; 58, Katherine Frey/The Washington Post/Getty Images; 59 (UP), Louisville MSD; 59 (LO), Chen Cheng/Xinhua/Alamy Live News/Alamy Stock Photo; 60, Mike Theiss/National Geographic Image Collection; 61 (UP), Photobank gallery/Shutterstock; 61 (LO), Yaya Ernst/Shutterstock

CHAPTER 4: 62-63, Mike Mezeul II; 64-65, Science History Images/Alamy Stock Photo; 65, Science History Images/Alamy Stock Photo; 66, Bill Brooks/Alamy Stock Photo; 67, Tony Moran/Shutterstock; 68 (LE), Feng Yu/Shutterstock; 68 (RT), SPL Creative RM/Getty Images; 70 (UP), NOAA; 70 (LO), NASA; 71 (LE), Mike Theiss/National Geographic Image Collection; 71 (RT), Ryan McGinnis/Getty Images; 72, Carsten Peter/National Geographic Image Collection; 73 (UP), John Warburton-Lee Photography/Alamy Stock Photo; 73 (LO), Dr. Joseph Golden/NOAA; 74, Ryan Soderlin/The World-Herald; 75 (UP LE), Carsten Peter/National Geographic Image Collection; 75 (UP RT), Johnny Goodson; 75 (CTR), Ana Filipa Scarpa/Mercury Press & Media/Caters News Agency; 75 (LO), Grant Hindsley/ZUMAPRESS.com/Alamy Stock Photo; 76, Frank Bienewald/Alamy Stock Photo; 77, John Sirlin/Alamy Stock Photo; 78 (UP), Bill Perry/Shutterstock; 78 (LO), kavram/iStockphoto/Getty Images; 79 (UP), Robert Clark/National Geographic Image Collection; 79 (CTR), Chun Guo/Dreamstime; 79 (LO), George Steinmetz/National Geographic Image Collection

CHAPTER 5: 80-81, Jerry Lampen/EPA-EFE/REX/Shutterstock; 82, Miguel Riopa/AFP/Getty Images; 83 (UP), Albert Gea/Reuters; 83 (CTR), Albert Gea/Reuters; 83 (LO), Miguel Riopa/AFP/Getty Images; 84, Jim Reed; 85, stanley45/iStockphoto; 86, mauritius images GmbH/Alamy Stock Photo; 87 (UP), imageBROKER/Alamy Stock Photo; 87 (LO RT), Carlos Aguilar/AFP/Getty Images; 87 (LO LE), Jeremy Richards/iStockphoto/Getty Images; 88, Erik S. Lesser/EPA/Shutterstock; 89 (UP), Sebastien Bozon/AFP/Getty Images; 89 (CTR), Minnitre/Shutterstock; 89 (LO), TriggerPhoto/iStockphoto/Getty Images; 90, Design Pics Inc/Alamy Stock Photo; 91 (UP), Lori Greig/Moment RF/Getty Images; 91 (LO), Vitaly Korovin/Shutterstock; 92, Gerd Ludwig/National Geographic Image Collection; 93, Jim Reed; 94, John Sirlin/Alamy Stock Photo; 95, Robert Estall photo agency/Alamy Stock Photo

CHAPTER 6: 96-97, blickwinkel/Alamy Stock Photo; 98, Linda Davidson/The Washington Post/Getty Images; 99 (UP), Jim Lo Scalzo/EPA/Shutterstock; 99 (CTR), Jewel Samad/AFP/Getty Images; 99 (LO), Nicholas Kamm/AFP/Getty Images; 100, VDABKK/Shutterstock; 101, Don Johnston_GA/Alamy Stock Photo; 102 (A), Ted M. Kinsman/Science Source; 102 (B, C), Kenneth Libbrecht/Science Source; 102 (D), Kichigin/Shutterstock; 103, John Burcham/National Geographic Image Collection;

270

CREDITS

Published by National Geographic Partners, LLC. All rights reserved. Reproduction of the whole or any part of the contents without written permission from the publisher is prohibited.

Since 1888, the National Geographic Society has funded more than 12,000 research, exploration, and preservation projects around the world. The Society receives funds from National Geographic Partners, LLC, funded in part by your purchase. A portion of the proceeds from this book supports this vital work. To learn more, visit natgeo.com/info.

NATIONAL GEOGRAPHIC and Yellow Border Design are trademarks of the National Geographic Society, used under license.

For more information, visit nationalgeographic.com, call 1-877-873-6846, or write to the following address:

National Geographic Partners
1145 17th Street N.W.
Washington, D.C. 20036-4688 U.S.A.

Visit us online at nationalgeographic.com/books

For librarians and teachers: ngchildrensbooks.org

More for kids from National Geographic: natgeokids.com

National Geographic Kids magazine inspires children to explore their world with fun yet educational articles on animals, science, nature, and more. Using fresh storytelling and amazing photography, Nat Geo Kids shows kids ages 6 to 14 the fascinating truth about the world—and why they should care. kids.nationalgeographic.com/subscribe

For information about special discounts for bulk purchases, please contact National Geographic Books Special Sales: specialsales@natgeo.com

For rights or permissions inquiries, please contact National Geographic Books Subsidiary Rights: bookrights@natgeo.com

Designed by Rachel Kenny

Hardcover ISBN: 978-1-4263-3543-3
Reinforced library binding ISBN: 978-1-4263-3544-0

The publisher would like to acknowledge the following people for making this book possible: Priyanka Lamichhane, senior editor; Jen Agresta, project editor; Stephanie Warren Drimmer, author; Sanjida Rashid, art director; Rachel Kenny, designer; Lori Epstein, photo director; Karen Kosiba, expert reviewer; Michelle Harris, fact-checker; Joan Gossett, editorial production manager; and Anne LeongSon and Gus Tello, design production assistants.

Printed in China
19/PPS/1

I DO NOT LIKE THAT NAME

Erin McGill

Greenwillow Books

An Imprint of HarperCollinsPublishers

One morning when Sophie and Herb were having breakfast, Sophie noticed something on the cereal box.

"Look at this, Herb! We can send away for an elephant," she said.

"Ohhh, that would be exciting!" said Herb.

"Can you imagine all the fun we could have with our very own elephant?"

"Let's do it!"
said Sophie.

"Before they run out of elephants!"
said Herb.

WIDE LOAD
HANDLE
FRAGILE
WITH CARE
PAC EXPRESS
WE STAMPEDE TO YOUR DOOR

Finally,
the big day arrived.

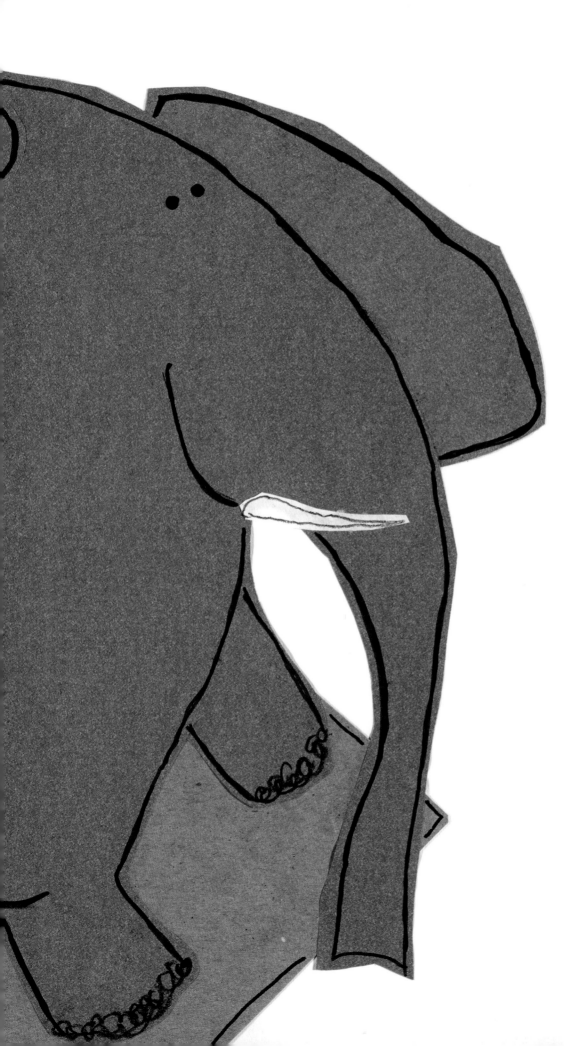

"I'm Sophie,"
said Sophie.
"What is
your name?"

"I don't have a name,"
said the elephant.

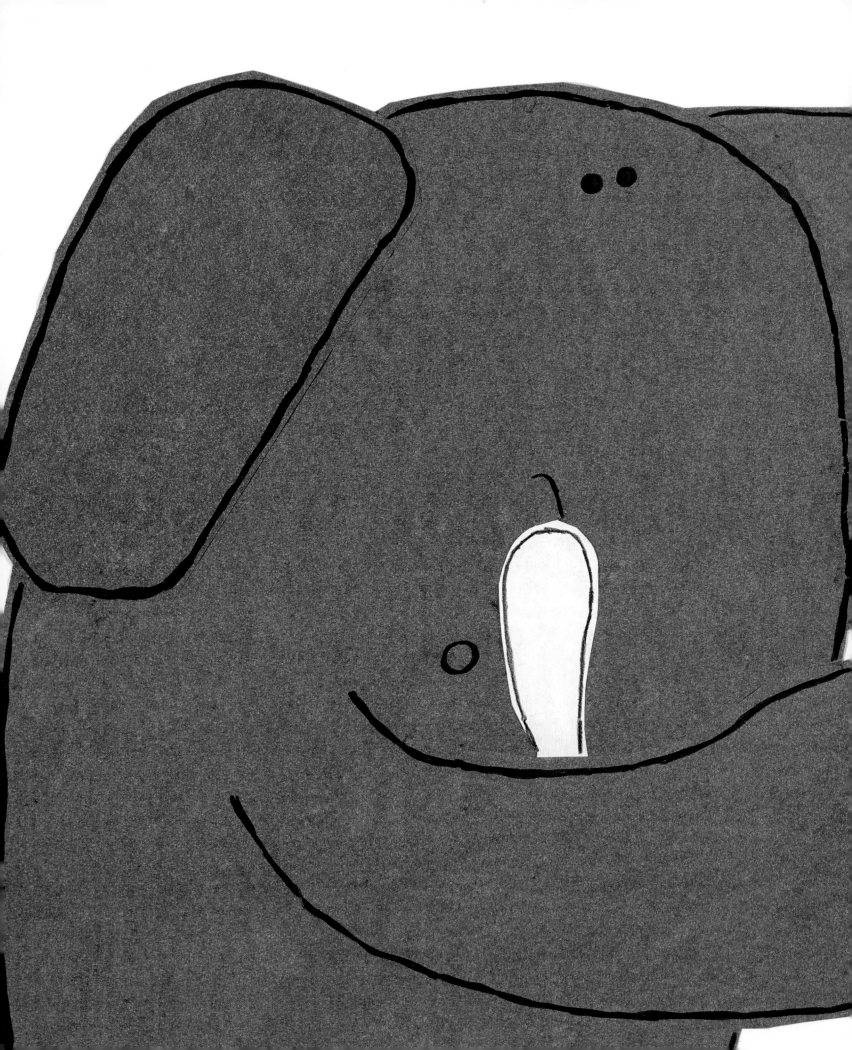

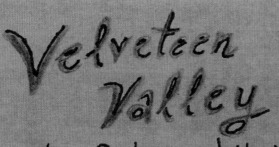

Ship to: Sophie and Herb's House

From: **PACHYDERM EXPRESS**

The premier elephant-delivery service

Enclosed is **1** elephant

To be named upon arrival

CONGRATULATIONS!

You have a new friend.

Thank you for your order. We at Velveteen Valley appreciate your business. Look for Peanut Crunch, our newest flavor. Perfect for elephants!

**"It's your job to name me,"
said the elephant.**

And it's how others know when something belongs to you.

"We will help you pick out the right name," said Herb.

"Ohhh, I know," said Sophie.
"I love flowers and ballet.
What about Petal or Buttercup
or Twinkle Toes?"

"I do not think so! I am not a flower and I am not light on my toes. I do not like those names," the elephant said.

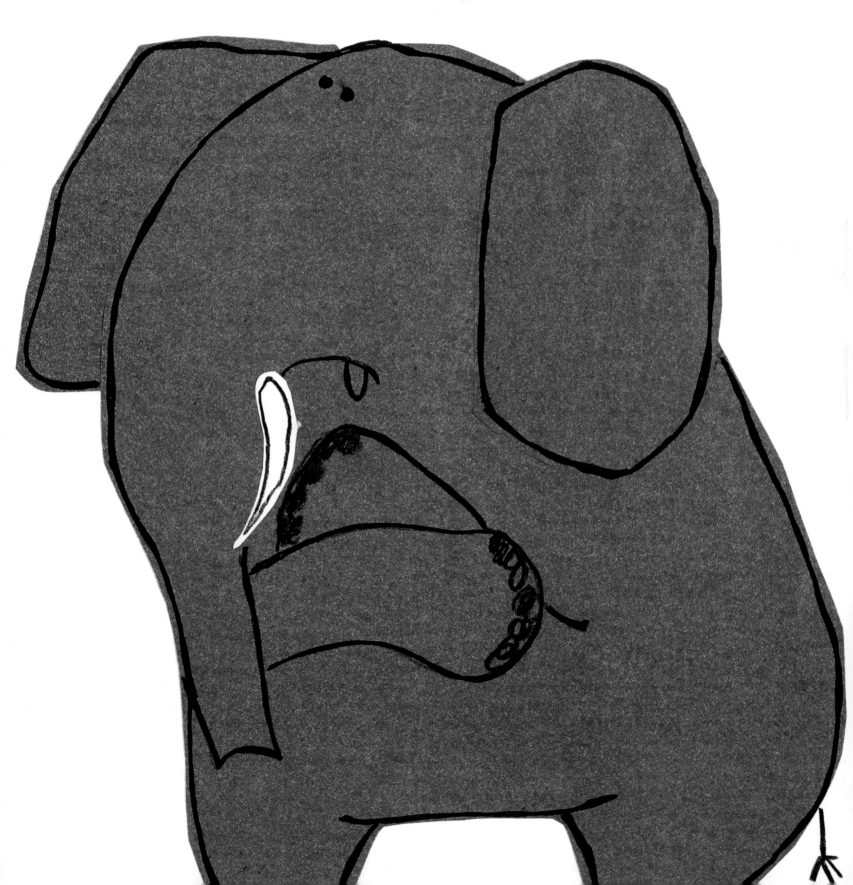

"Hmmm . . . Marshmallow, maybe?
String Bean? Or what about
Sweet Potato?" said Herb.

"No way! I do not like those names, either! I want a name that's right for me. How did you get your names?" asked the elephant.

"I come from a long line of Herbs," said Herb.

"And I am named after a famous ballerina," said Sophie.

The elephant remembered an elephant from long, long ago named Tony the Woolly.

"Tony the Woolly was heroic, noble, adventurous, and smart, just like me," he told Sophie and Herb.

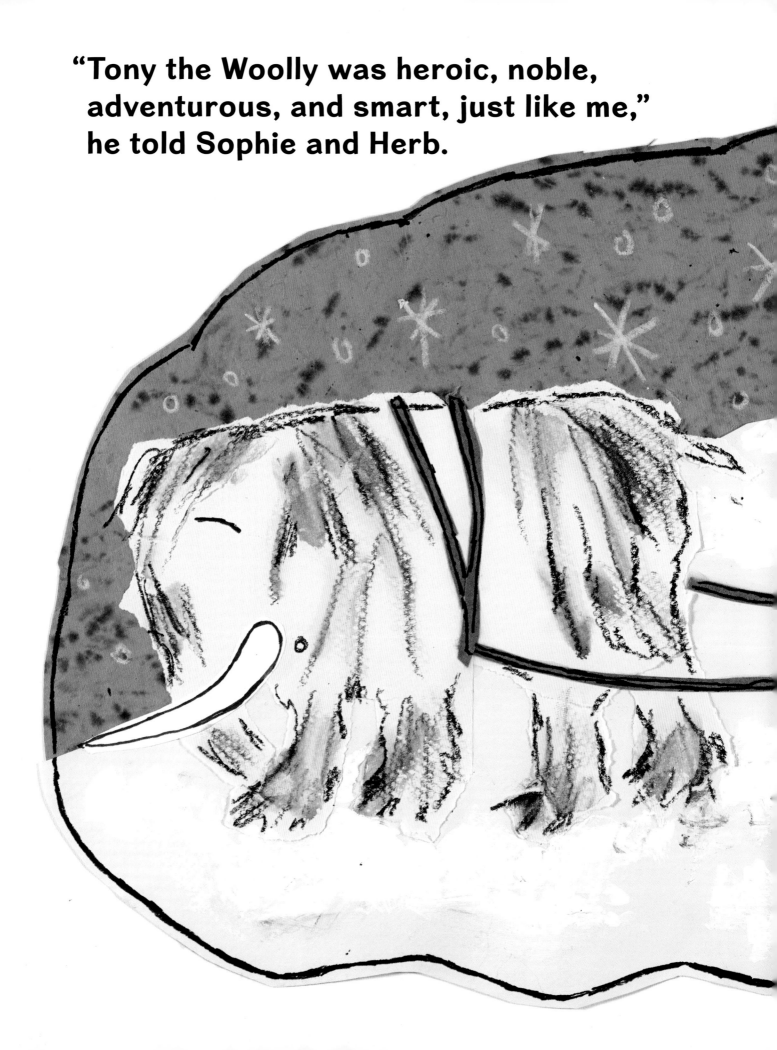

"I like the name Tony," he said.
"It is too bad that I am not woolly."

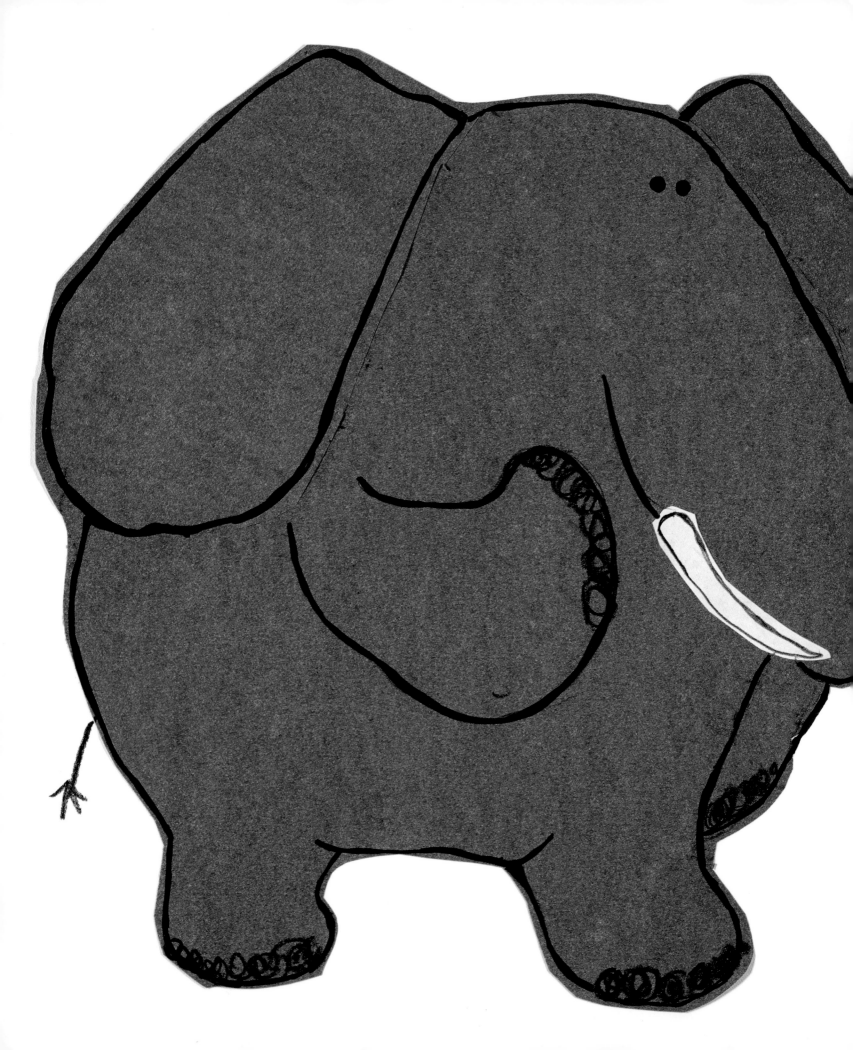

"The best part
of having a name is
making it your own,"
said Sophie.

"Come on, Tony, let's go
have some fun!" said Herb.

"That sounds just right to me,"
said Tony.
"Hooray for our friend Tony!"
said Sophie and Herb.

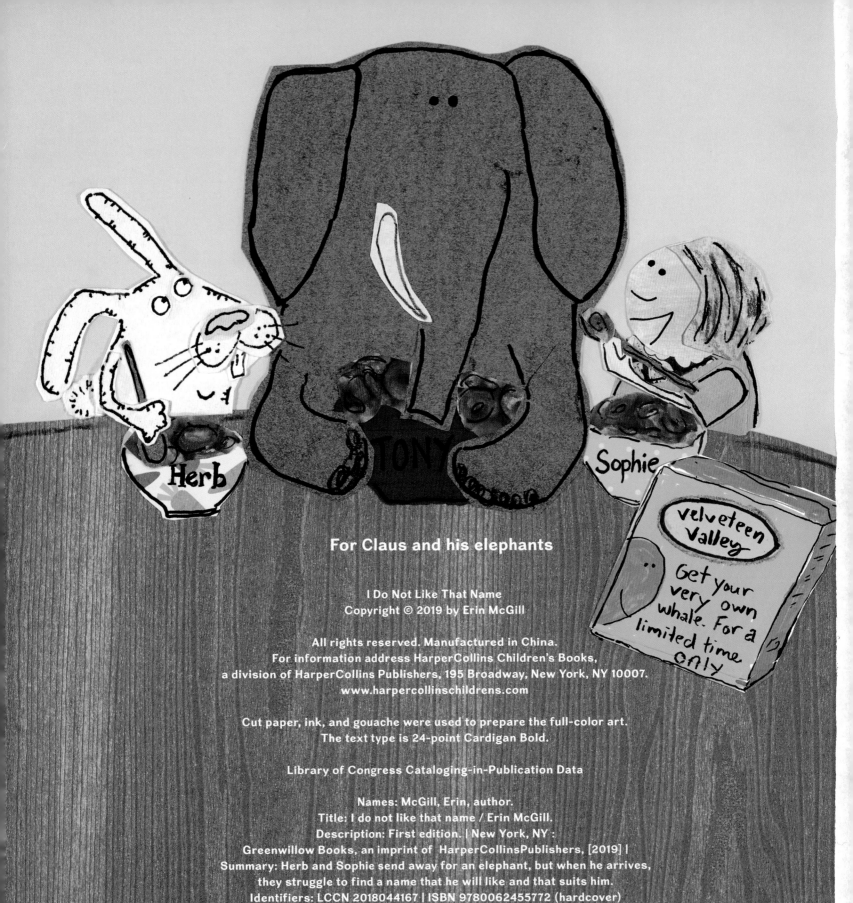

For Claus and his elephants

Cut paper, ink, and gouache were used to prepare the full-color art.
The text type is 24-point Cardigan Bold.

Library of Congress Cataloging-in-Publication Data

Names: McGill, Erin, author.
Title: I do not like that name / Erin McGill.
Description: First edition. | New York, NY :
Greenwillow Books, an imprint of HarperCollinsPublishers, [2019] |
Summary: Herb and Sophie send away for an elephant, but when he arrives,
they struggle to find a name that he will like and that suits him.
Identifiers: LCCN 2018044167 | ISBN 9780062455772 (hardcover)
Subjects: | CYAC: Names, Personal—Fiction. | Elephants—Fiction. | Humorous stories.
Classification: LCC PZ7.1.M43515 Iar 2019 | DDC [E]—dc23 LC record available at https://lccn.loc.gov/2018044167

19 20 21 22 23 SCP 10 9 8 7 6 5 4 3 2 1
First Edition

Greenwillow Books